$\mathcal{D}$

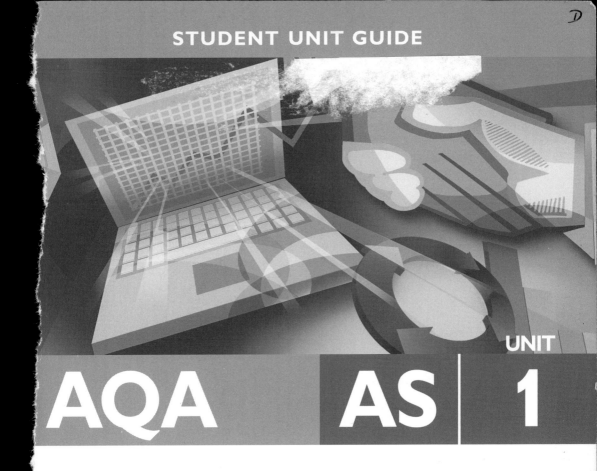

AQA

AS

1

Business Studies

Planning and Financing a Business

John Wolinski

Philip Allan Updates, an imprint of Hodder Education, part of Hachette UK, Market Place, Deddington, Oxfordshire OX15 0SE

Orders

Bookpoint Ltd, 130 Milton Park, Abingdon, Oxfordshire OX14 4SB
tel: 01235 827720
fax: 01235 400454
e-mail: uk.orders@bookpoint.co.uk
Lines are open 9.00 a.m.–5.00 p.m., Monday to Saturday, with a 24-hour message answering service. You can also order through the Philip Allan Updates website: www.philipallan.co.uk

© Philip Allan Updates 2008

ISBN 978-0-340-94791-3

First printed 2008
Impression number 5 4 3 2
Year 2013 2012 2011 2010 2009

This guide has been written specifically to support students preparing for the AQA AS Business Studies Unit 1 examination. The content has been neither approved nor endorsed by AQA and remains the sole responsibility of the author.

Typeset by DC Graphic Design, Swanley Village, Kent
Printed by MPG Books, Bodmin

Hachette UK's policy is to use papers that are natural, renewable and recyclable products and made from wood grown in sustainable forests. The logging and manufacturing processes are expected to conform to the environmental regulations of the country of origin.

P01299

Contents

Introduction

■ ■ ■

Content Guidance

■ ■ ■

Questions and Answers

Introduction

About this guide

This guide has been written with one objective in mind: to provide you with the ideal resource for your revision of AQA AS Business Studies Unit 1 — BUSS1 — Planning and Financing a Business. After this introduction on the aims and assessment of AS, the guide is divided into two sections: Content Guidance and Questions and Answers.

The Content Guidance section offers concise coverage of Unit 1, combining an overview of key terms and concepts with an identification of opportunities for you to illustrate the higher-level skills of analysis and evaluation. The scope for linking different topic areas is also shown.

The Question and Answer section provides six case studies, which are focused on specific areas of content and in the same order as the first section. Case study 1 combines the first three topics of the 'Planning and Financing a Business' unit of the AQA specification: 'Enterprise', 'Generating and protecting business ideas' and 'Transforming resources into goods and services'. Case studies 2 and 3 then deal with the remaining sections in order, with the exception of 'Raising finance'. Case studies 4 and 5 cover 'Raising finance', along with the second element of the Unit 1 specification, 'Financial planning'.

The Question and Answer section concludes with case study 6. This is a fully integrated case study, for final revision purposes. Although the previous five case studies are presented in exactly the same way as an AQA Unit 1 paper, they are designed to support your revision of specific areas of the specification, so they deliberately cover a limited number of topics. Case study 6, however, takes the format of an actual Unit 1 examination paper because it includes topics from across the whole specification.

Each question is based on the format of the AS papers. Case studies 1, 2, 4 and 6 are followed by two sample answers (an A-grade and a lower-grade response) interspersed by examiner comments. Case studies 3 and 5 are followed by a sample A-grade answer.

You should read through the relevant topic area in the Content Guidance section before attempting any question from the Question and Answer section, and only read the specimen answers after you have tackled the question yourself. The Unit 1 examination consists of a mix of compulsory questions based on a mini-case study, ranging from short-answer questions to extended responses. The time allocation for Unit 1 is 75 minutes (1 hour 15 minutes). After reading time of approximately 10 minutes, you are advised to spend 20 minutes answering question 1 (short answers) and between 40 and 45 minutes on question 2 (extended responses).

Aims of the AS qualification

AQA AS Business Studies aims to encourage candidates to develop a critical understanding of the following:
- the importance of entrepreneurial activity in the UK
- the issues involved in business start-ups, such as research and planning and sound financial management
- the factors that determine success in small and expanding businesses
- the internal functions of contemporary business organisations of all types
- how established businesses might improve their effectiveness by making tactical decisions at a functional level

In addition, the specification has been designed to encourage students to acquire a range of important and transferable skills, useful in both future employment and higher education:
- data skills — students will be expected to manipulate data in a variety of forms and to interpret their results
- presenting arguments and making judgements and justified recommendations on the basis of the available evidence
- recognising the nature of problems, solving problems and making decisions using appropriate business tools and methods
- planning work, taking into account the demands of the task and the time available to complete it
- conducting research into a specific theme in preparation for one or more tasks
- challenging their own assumptions using evidence that has become available

Unit 1: Planning and financing a business

Specifically, this unit provides an introduction to the scope of business studies in the context of starting a new business. It is intended to develop understanding of:
- the range of activities involved in setting up a small business
- the key financial concepts essential for the planning of small businesses

These business activities are considered primarily in terms of their role in the *planning* and *establishing* of a new business, as opposed to the actual operation of an existing business.

Assessment

AS and A2 papers are designed to test certain skills. Every mark that is awarded on an AS or A2 paper is given for the demonstration of a skill. The content of the course (the theories, concepts and ideas) provides a framework to allow students to show their skills — recognising the content on its own is not enough to merit high marks.

The following skills are tested:
- **Knowledge and understanding** — recognising and describing business concepts and ideas.

- **Application** — being able to explain or apply your understanding.
- **Analysis** — developing a line of thought in order to demonstrate its impact or consequences.
- **Evaluation** — making a judgement by weighing up the evidence provided.

Unit 1 is weighted so that, on average, marks for each question paper are awarded as follows:

	Weighting	
Knowledge	21	How well you know the meanings, theories and ideas
Application	16/17	How well you can explain benefits, problems, calculations, situations
Analysis	12	How well you develop ideas and apply theory and ideas to matters
Evaluation*	10/11	How well you show judgement, such as the overall significance of the situation
Total	60 marks	

* Marks awarded for evaluation incorporate an allocation of marks for quality of language.

Unit 1 has a lower weighting for the 'higher-level' skills of analysis and evaluation, in comparison to the other three A-level papers, as it is designed to be the paper that begins the process of the transition from GCSE to A-level. However, you should bear in mind that the AS course focuses on developing arguments more fully than GCSEs. Consequently, during your preparation and revision for Unit 1, you will need to practise developing arguments more fully. This will also be good practice for Unit 2 and the A2 papers, which have a higher weighting than Unit 1 for both analysis and evaluation. The units have been designed to allow you to develop skills, especially evaluation, as you progress through the course.

For the purposes of comparison, the 80 marks awarded for the Unit 2 paper are allocated as follows:

	Weighting	
Knowledge	21	How well you know the meanings, theories and ideas
Application	19	How well you can explain benefits, problems, calculations, situations
Analysis	23	How well you develop ideas and apply theory and ideas to matters
Evaluation*	17	How well you show judgement, such as the overall significance of the situation
Total	80 marks	

* Marks awarded for evaluation incorporate an allocation of marks for quality of language.

Skills requirement of a question

A rough guide to the skills requirement of a question is its mark allocation. In the case of Unit 1 (75 minutes), 60 marks are available. After approximately 10 minutes for reading the text and the questions, this is just over 1 mark a minute. Use this as a guide to the time you spend on each question, but allow some flexibility in your planning. For individual questions the mark allocation will tend to be as follows:

2–3 marks	A definition or description showing knowledge*
4–7 marks	An explanation or calculation showing application*
8–11 marks	Development of an argument in the context of the question showing analysis**
12–18 marks	A judgement of a situation or proposed action showing evaluation**

* Question 1 is a 5- or 6-part question consisting of shorter tasks that require knowledge and application only.

** Question 2 is a 3-part question consisting of extended responses that require analysis and evaluation.

In the assessment of 'higher-level' questions requiring analysis or evaluation, marks will also be given for the other skills. Factual knowledge displayed, for example, will earn marks for *knowledge* (content), and explanations and calculations will be awarded *application* marks.

A more specific guide to the skills requirement of a question is to look at the trigger word introducing the question. Specific trigger words tend to be used to show you when you are being asked to analyse or evaluate. For AS, these are generally as follows:

Analyse
- 'Analyse...'
- 'Explain why...'
- 'Examine...'
- 'Consider...'

Evaluate
- 'Evaluate...'
- 'Discuss...'
- 'To what extent...?'
- 'Justify....'

If these trigger words are missing on an AS paper, you are probably being asked to show 'lower-level' skills, i.e. knowledge of the specification content or application (explanation).

On financial questions, the recall of a formula or method of calculation (e.g. breakeven quantity) is knowledge. Carrying out calculations is application. This means that the high-mark questions that test analysis and evaluation will not usually involve calculations. Focus on understanding the purposes and limitations of the financial elements of the course and you will be well prepared for these questions. That said, analysis questions may well require you to interpret the meaning of a calculation.

Students who fail to *analyse* generally do so because they have curtailed their argument. The words and phrases below serve to provide logical links in an argument:

- 'and so...'
- 'which will mean/lead to...'
- 'because...'
- 'and this will affect...'

By using them, you can demonstrate your ability to analyse. Always ask yourself: 'am I explaining *why*?'

In order to *evaluate*, you need to demonstrate judgement and the ability to reach a reasoned conclusion. The following terms will demonstrate to the examiner that this is your intention:

- 'The most significant...is...because...'
- 'However, ...would also need to be considered because...'
- 'The probable result is...because...'
- 'On balance...because...'

The suggestions above are only a few of the many ways in which judgements can be shown, but note the importance of the word 'because'.

Opportunities for evaluation in Unit 1

What follows is a summary of many of the probable opportunities for the demonstration of evaluation in Unit 1, although it is not an exhaustive list. The structure of the unit and the nature of the topics mean that there are more opportunities in the 'Starting a business' section than in the 'Financial planning' part of the specification, although there are many opportunities for application in the financial elements. The list does not include possibilities for evaluation that might arise from combining different areas of the specification in an evaluative question. The nature of the topics also means that there are many opportunities for evaluation that might arise from combining the different areas, such as the impact of a location decision on budgeting or the implications of extensive market research on cash flow in both the short run and the long run.

The summary below does not include the potential for this type of integration. In many instances, evaluation can be improved by referring to the effect of an issue from one topic area on a different aspect of the organisation. Indeed, close examination of any issue may show how difficult it is to find a business problem within the scope of Unit 1 that does *not* integrate with other elements of the unit.

Starting a business

Opportunities for evaluation are:

- assessing a balance between risk and reward in a particular business start-up
- judging the importance of different characteristics of the entrepreneur in terms of their influence on the business's achievements
- evaluating the significance of different motives for becoming an entrepreneur
- viewing the significance of the entrepreneur's skills, relative to other factors that influence the success of a new business
- the relative merits of a franchise as opposed to an independent start-up
- the overall impact of a patent or copyright on the business's financial success
- discussion of the main factors that lead to a business adding value
- the relative merits of different sources of information in constructing a sound business plan
- the importance of the business plan to the business
- evaluating the strengths and weaknesses of a particular business plan
- advising on how a business plan might be improved
- the relative merits of different forms of market research, such as primary v. secondary or qualitative v. quantitative
- an overall assessment of the quality of market research conducted by a new entrepreneur
- judgement of the strengths and weaknesses of the sampling methods chosen in a new business start-up
- the relative importance of different factors that influence the demand for the business's products or services
- weighing up the benefits and problems involved in using market segmentation
- the significance of limited liability for a business
- discussion of the relative merits of different forms of legal structure for a business in a particular situation
- assessing the pros and cons of different sources of finance for a start-up business
- appreciating the need to modify a business's choice of how to raise finance in the light of changing circumstances
- recognising the relative importance of different factors influencing start-up location decisions
- appreciating the relative merits of full-time and part-time or temporary and permanent employees in different situations
- evaluating situations in which the use of consultants and advisers is particularly useful

Financial planning

Opportunities for evaluation are:
- interpreting the extent to which changes in costs and/or revenue can impact upon profit
- recognising situations in which changes in profit arising from changes in output can be greatly influenced by the balance of fixed and variable costs
- awareness of the strengths and weaknesses of breakeven analysis
- making decisions on whether to start a business based on contribution calculations and/or breakeven analysis

- evaluating the best sources of information for cash-flow forecasts
- understanding the significance of the data in a cash-flow forecast
- assessing the usefulness of a cash-flow forecast to the business
- evaluating the usefulness of planning budgets
- arguing the relative importance of the different reasons for setting a budget, in a particular situation
- evaluating the main problems in setting a budget
- judging whether a financial trend (e.g. cash flow) is within a firm's control
- weighing up the most likely causes of potential difficulties indicated by a cash-flow forecast and/or budget
- showing awareness of the main objectives of a particular start-up
- judging the overall success of a start-up by comparing its performance with its objectives
- comparing and contrasting the main risks involved in a particular start-up
- evaluating the strengths and weaknesses of a specific business idea
- drawing a conclusion about the main reasons why a business start-up may fail or may have failed
- recognising the extent to which a business's success or failure has depended on factors within or outside the business's control

Revision strategies

Below is a list of general pieces of advice for exam preparation.
- Prepare well in advance.
- Organise your files, ensuring there are no gaps in your notes.
- Prepare a list of key terms/definitions in readiness for the exam. Defining a term in an exam immediately shows that you understand the concept or topic, and it can help to clarify your arguments.
- Read different approaches. There is no one right approach to business studies. Experience as many views and methods as possible. Read newspapers and business articles.
- When reading an article, try to think of the types of question an examiner might ask and how you would answer them. Remember, some of your examination questions will be based on actual organisations.
- Take notes as you read. These will help you to:
  - put the text into your own words, cementing your understanding
  - summarise and emphasise the key points
  - focus your attention
  - précis information that could help with future revision
  - boost your morale by showing an end product of your revision sessions
- Develop and use your higher-level skills. Make sure that your revision is not dominated by factual knowledge only. Check that you can explain and analyse the points noted, and try to imagine situations in which evaluation can be applied.
- Practise examination questions. Use the questions in this book (and specimen and past papers from the AQA website) to improve your technique, making sure that

you complete them in the time allowed. In the examination, you must complete two multi-part questions in 75 minutes. A 75-minute examination paper means that there is a reasonable but finite amount of time to develop your answers. You must make sure that you have enough time to evaluate the final part of question 2. Remember that, within a question, the later parts carry more marks and therefore need longer, more fully developed answers. Remember, after reading time the 60 marks awarded approximate to 1 mark per minute. Use this as a guide to the time you need to spend on a particular question.

- Maintain your motivation. Reward yourself for achieving targets, but do not get demoralised if you fall behind. If necessary, amend your objectives to a more realistic level.
- Find out the dates and times of your examinations and use this to prepare a detailed schedule for the study leave/examination period, making sure you build in time for relaxation and sleep.
- Focus on all areas of the specification rather than just your favourite topics. Your revision is more likely to 'add value' if it improves your understanding of a problem area. Revising a topic that you already know is a morale booster, but is it as valuable?
- Top up your memory just before the examination. If there are concepts, formulae or ratios that you find difficult, revisit them just before the examination.
- Adopt your own strategies. Everyone has different learning styles — use the approach or methods that work for you.

Using the Question and Answer section

You can use the final section of this guide as an integral part of your revision. The questions are based on the format of the Unit 1 examination paper. The usual pattern is for each mini case study to be followed by two multi-part questions.

Question 1 is a five- or six-part question consisting of shorter tasks that require knowledge and application only.

Question 2 is a three-part question consisting of extended responses that require analysis and evaluation.

A common problem for students (and teachers) on completing a topic is the lack of examination questions that cover only that area. The questions in this guide are tailored so that you can apply your learning while a topic is still fresh in your mind, either during the course or when you have revised a topic in preparation for the examination.

Caution: although you may cover the topics within a few weeks of starting the course, it is unlikely that you will be able to develop fully the higher-level skills of evaluation. For this reason, you are advised not to attempt these questions too early in the course. However, you may find it helpful to read a sample A-grade response.

Content
Guidance

This section of the guide outlines the topic areas of Unit 1, which are as follows:
- Starting a business
- Financial planning

Read through the relevant topic area before attempting a question from the Question and Answer section.

Key terms

Key terms are either defined or shown in **bold**. You should also have a business studies dictionary to hand.

Analysis

Under this heading, there are suggestions on how topic areas could lend themselves to analysis. During your course and the revision period, you should refer to these opportunities. Test and practise your understanding of the variety of ways in which a logical argument or line of reasoning can be developed.

Evaluation

Under this heading, general opportunities for evaluation are highlighted within particular topic areas. A wide range of 'Opportunities for evaluation' are described in the Introduction.

Integration

Under the heading 'Links', the scope for linking different topic areas is shown. Most business problems have many dimensions and a student who can show, for example, the effect of a business's location on its budgeting will be rewarded. Look for these opportunities to integrate. Unit 1 focuses on a business start-up, so the business plan provides an integrating theme throughout Unit 1. A successful start-up will require careful planning in every aspect of the business, so throughout the unit there are opportunities to bring topic areas together. This integration culminates in the final topic, 'Assessing business start-ups', which brings the whole of Unit 1 together in order to evaluate the start-ups' potential for success.

Starting a business

Enterprise

Enterprise and entrepreneurs

Key terms

enterprise: almost any business or organisation can be called an enterprise, but the term usually refers to the process by which new businesses are formed and new products and services are created and brought to the market. Enterprises are usually led by an entrepreneur

enterprise skills: skills that allow an individual or organisation to respond effectively to changing market situations. They include problem-solving skills, thinking and acting innovatively and creatively, and understanding the importance of risk and uncertainty. The definition of enterprise capability used by the Department for Children, Schools and Families (DCSF) (formerly the Department for Education and Skills, DfES) includes the following skills: innovation, creativity, risk management, risk taking and a can-do attitude.

entrepreneurs: individuals who have an idea that they develop by setting up a new business and encouraging it to grow. They take the risk and the subsequent profits that come with success, or the losses that come with failure.

The characteristics of successful entrepreneurs include:

- willingness to take risks — this is probably the most important quality of an entrepreneur
- ability to spot and take advantage of opportunities
- determination and persistence
- passion
- relevant skills and expertise — some surveys suggest that this is the key factor influencing the success of small businesses, as it is crucial for the quality of service provided
- vision, creativity and innovation
- motivation to succeed and not be daunted by failure

Having an entrepreneurial attitude is vitally important in today's job market for the following reasons:

- Individuals change jobs more often.
- Management structures have become less formal and more flexible.
- Working methods have become more interactive.
- Businesses are more likely to encourage individuals to spot opportunities, take initiatives and adapt to changing circumstances.

Importance of risk and rewards such as profit

In the UK, over one-third of people surveyed say that they are afraid of failure — quite naturally, as the majority of new businesses fail. Failure occurs for a number of reasons:

- lack of finance
- poor infrastructure
- skills shortages
- complexity of regulations or 'red tape'

The ability to evaluate the risks and uncertainty that are an integral part of almost all business decisions is an important element of successful enterprise. An entrepreneur who can overcome risks will be rewarded with the profit that the business earns. Many people avoid risks, so there are often high profits to be made from a business idea that competitors are afraid to exploit.

Opportunity cost

This is the 'real cost' of taking a particular action or the next best alternative forgone, i.e. the next best thing that could have been chosen but was not. For example, the opportunity cost of setting up a new business might be the wage from her old job that an entrepreneur gives up.

Motives for becoming an entrepreneur

It is estimated that between 400,000 and 500,000 new businesses start up each year. Motives for becoming an entrepreneur vary from the existence of favourable circumstances that will help an entrepreneur to set up, to personal factors that might encourage individuals to set up their own business.

Reasons include:

- government encouragement of people to be more entrepreneurial (e.g. enterprise education in schools)
- increasing wealth, which gives people more business opportunities and less risk
- the pace of change, which is constantly creating new opportunities
- the desire for more independence at work
- a wish to make money
- a desire to use a talent or skill in a useful and profitable way
- attempting to provide employment or wealth for the local area

Government support for enterprise and entrepreneurs

Governments support enterprise for several reasons:

- to provide more products and services for communities
- to reduce unemployment by allowing more firms to become established
- to fill market niches and so satisfy certain tastes — this also gives more choice to customers

- to help productivity to improve by increasing competitive pressures in markets
- to encourage more flexible businesses that support the introduction of new ideas and technologies and more efficient working practices

The Enterprise Directorate (previously the Small Business Service) in the Department of Business, Enterprise and Regulatory Reform (DBERR, formerly the Department of Trade and Industry) is the government's expert policy unit on small business issues.

Government support is provided by:
- reducing business taxes and trying to establish and maintain a modern and competitive business tax system
- reducing the burden of regulations and bureaucracy on enterprises
- reducing barriers to raising finance for small businesses
- improving the support for small and new businesses
- promoting a change in the UK's enterprise culture
- encouraging business start-ups in economically deprived regions of the UK
- introducing legislation to promote competition
- funding projects to raise awareness of enterprise among under-represented groups of people
- encouraging unemployed people to move into self-employment

Analysis
Opportunities for analysis are:
- examining the skills or characteristics needed by an entrepreneur
- assessing weaknesses in an entrepreneur
- analysing the reasons for a business failure
- recognising the opportunity cost of a business decision
- showing understanding of the motives of a particular entrepreneur
- explaining reasons for government support for enterprise
- indicating how government support can help entrepreneurs

Evaluation
Opportunities for evaluation are:
- assessing a balance between risk and reward in a particular business start-up
- evaluating the risks and rewards to an entrepreneur
- judging the importance of different characteristics of the entrepreneur in terms of their influence on the business's achievements
- evaluating the significance of different motives for becoming an entrepreneur
- viewing the significance of the entrepreneur's skills, relative to other factors that influence the success of a new business

Links
This topic links with *all* of the other elements of Unit 1. The major links are:
- the skills of the entrepreneur in providing an idea or identifying a suitable product or market niche

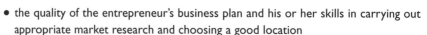

- the quality of the entrepreneur's business plan and his or her skills in carrying out appropriate market research and choosing a good location
- the need for an entrepreneur to raise sufficient finance to develop the business and his or her skills in areas of financial planning such as cash-flow forecasting and budgeting
- the importance of the entrepreneur's skills when assessing the relative success of a business start-up

Generating and protecting business ideas

Sources of business ideas

Ideas can be generated by the process of brainstorming or can come from the entrepreneur's own personal and/or business experience.

Research suggests that there are four major sources of ideas for entrepreneurs:
- spotting trends and anticipating their impact on people's lives (e.g. mobile communication technology)
- noticing something that is missing from the market or that can be improved on (e.g. online holiday bookings)
- copying ideas from other countries (e.g. car valeting)
- taking a scientific approach (e.g. Dyson's cyclonic cleaner)

Other sources include:
- brainstorming (e.g. Innocent when considering new flavours)
- personal/business experience (e.g. Liftshare — a car-sharing service used by the Glastonbury Festival)

Identification of a product or market niche

Once a business has used these methods, it needs to identify both the product itself and the market niche that it will target. Looking at each of the sources above, the business must then plan its actions carefully.
- Spotting trends: the business must decide on the exact style of product that meets this market's needs.
- Noticing something that is missing: what product or service best fits this gap?
- Copying ideas from other countries: will the same customers be targeted in the UK?
- Taking a scientific approach: the product is decided, but who will buy it?
- Brainstorming: again, an idea of the potential market is needed.
- Personal/business experience: how relevant is the experience? Does the idea need to be adapted to the market?

Franchising

A franchise is when a business (the franchisor) gives the right to supply its product or service to another business (the franchisee).

Types of franchise

- **Business format franchise.** This is when the owner of a business (the franchisor) grants a licence to another person or business (the franchisee) to use their business idea — often in a specific geographical area. The franchisee sells the franchisor's products or services, trades under the franchisor's trademark or tradename, and benefits from the franchisor's help and support.
- **Distributorship and dealership.** Here the franchisee sells the products but does not usually trade under the franchise name. In this case, the franchisee has more freedom over how they run their business. This is common in car sales, where a particular showroom may be the main dealership for, say, Toyota cars.
- **Agency.** This is where the franchisee sells goods or services on behalf of the supplier (franchisor).
- **Licensing.** Here the franchisee has a licence giving them the right to make and sell the licensor's product. Like distributorships and dealerships, there are usually no extra restrictions on how the business is run.

Benefits to the franchisee of operating a franchise

- Franchises offer the lowest risk for a start-up business, and as a result a high percentage of them are successful.
- Franchise businesses usually have established brand names.
- Consequently, financing the business may be easier as banks may be more willing to lend money.
- The franchisee is likely to benefit from any national advertising or promotion by the franchisor.
- The franchisee will usually have a monopoly in their area.
- Relationships with suppliers are likely to have been established by the franchisor.
- The franchisor offers support and training.

Benefits to the franchisor of operating a franchise

- The franchisor receives a regular reward for the idea; the franchisee provides the capital and takes the risk.
- Rapid expansion is easier because the franchisor does not need to invest in additional premises etc.
- This helps the business to capture a larger share of the market more quickly.
- The franchisor retains control over the quality of the products and services, and the way they are marketed and distributed.

Disadvantages to the franchisee of operating a franchise

- There is a possibility that the franchisor has not set up a viable business idea.
- Costs may be higher than expected.

- The reduced risk of operating a franchise business may be set against lower financial rewards.
- Other franchisees could give the brand a bad reputation, and this may have an adverse impact on all franchisees.
- The franchise agreement usually includes restrictions on how the business should be run, reducing the owner's independence.
- It may be difficult to sell a franchise because the franchisor must agree to any new franchisee.

Disadvantages to the franchisor of operating a franchise

- The reputation of the business can be damaged by the actions of a single franchisee.
- It can be expensive to monitor all the franchisees.
- The profit from the franchisor's idea is being shared with the franchisees.

Protecting a business idea

Business ideas can be protected by using copyright, patents and trademarks.

Copyright

This is legal protection against copying for authors, composers and artists.

Copyright material includes:
- books
- information leaflets
- films
- computer programs
- sound recordings

The owner of the copyright can decide whether material can be copied. They can charge a royalty or licence fee.

Patents

A patent is an official document granting the holder the right to be the only user or producer of a newly invented product or process for a specified period.

If an individual invents a new process, piece of equipment, component or product, they may apply for a patent in order to prevent other people copying their invention and then making, selling, importing or using it without permission.

The Copyright, Designs and Patents Act 1988 gives patent holders the monopoly right to use, make, license or sell the invention for up to 20 years after it has been registered.

The benefits of patents are:
- The owner has a monopoly and can sell the product without close competition for up to 20 years.

- Having a patent means that the invention becomes the property of the inventor. A patent can be sold, rented or licensed, and so can bring in revenue, even if the inventor does not develop it themselves.
- A small business with an existing patent might become an attractive proposition for a large firm to purchase, simply in order to obtain the patent.

However:

- It costs a lot of money and takes a long time to apply for and protect a patent.
- Preventing other firms from using your patent can mean high legal costs.

Trademarks

These are signs, logos, symbols or words displayed on a company's products or on its advertising, including sounds or music, which distinguish its brands from those of its competitors. Trademarks can help a business by:

- providing an image that is instantly recognisable to customers
- creating a USP (unique selling point) by differentiating a product from those of its competitors
- making it easier to launch new products, using the widely recognised trademark

It may also be possible to earn money by selling a popular trademark to another business.

Analysis

Opportunities for analysis are:

- comparing different sources of business ideas in a specific firm
- recognising the impact of limited resources on the creation of business ideas
- linking the choice of product to the market niche targeted by the business
- assessing the benefits to the franchisor or franchisee of using a franchise
- assessing the drawbacks to the franchisor or franchisee of using a franchise
- explaining the benefits and/or drawbacks of copyright, patents and trademarks

Evaluation

Opportunities for evaluation are:

- the relative merits of a franchise as opposed to an independent start-up
- the overall impact of a patent or copyright on a business's financial success
- the weighing-up of two alternative franchises
- the key factors to consider when deciding on patenting/copyrighting/franchising

Links

This section links to the characteristics of the entrepreneur who has generated the business idea. Issues such as franchises and patents also link to market share and have an impact upon (and are influenced by) the level of finance available to a business start-up. The section 'Assessing business start-ups' relates closely to the belief that franchises or businesses that can protect an idea (e.g. through a patent) are likely to be less risky.

Transforming resources into goods and services

Inputs, outputs and the transformation process

Resources (inputs)

In order to produce goods and services, a business needs to use resources. These resources are the **inputs** into the production process, but are more commonly known as the **factors of production**.

resources or inputs: the elements that go into producing goods and services.
factors of production: the categorisation of the resources used to convert inputs into outputs, into four distinct elements — land, labour, capital and enterprise.

- **Land.** The term 'land' incorporates all the natural resources that can be used for production. Examples are land, mineral resources (e.g. coal and gold), livestock and fish.
- **Labour.** 'Labour' describes both the physical and mental effort involved in production. It therefore includes all types of jobs.
- **Capital.** Capital means goods that are made in order to produce other goods and services. Examples are machinery, computer systems, lorries and factories.
- **Enterprise.** Enterprise is the act of bringing together the other factors of production in order to create goods and services. This function is carried out by the entrepreneur, who makes decisions and provides the finance.

Improving the efficiency of the factors of production

There are a number of ways in which the efficiency of factors of production can be improved. Examples are:
- improving the fertility of land (e.g. through the use of fertilisers)
- using renewable or recyclable resources (this reduces waste)
- greater education and training of the workforce (to gain greater output from each employee)
- increasing the level of investment in capital equipment, as high-quality capital can improve the speed of production
- improvements in entrepreneurial skills and a willingness of entrepreneurs to take risks
- extending the overall scale of production (this should lead to greater efficiencies, such as bulk-buying)

The nature of output

The process by which inputs of factors of production are transformed into outputs is known as **production**.

content guidance

production: the process whereby resources (factors of production) are converted into a form that is intended to satisfy the requirements of potential customers.

It is important to note that the customer may be another firm and that production means providing services as well as making physical goods.

Inputs to outputs: the transformation process

The purpose of a business is to produce goods or services. In order to achieve this purpose a business must acquire inputs, convert them into outputs, and ensure that they reach the customer. All of these activities are part of the **transformation process**.

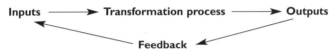

Figure 1 The transformation process

In the primary and secondary sectors, the part of 'land' which is raw materials is used up during the transformation process. In contrast, the remaining inputs remain intact and can be used again and again.

In the tertiary sector, the transformation process focuses directly on the consumer. No physical product emerges at the end of the process, but the consumer has experienced a change.

Classifying outputs

The main outputs of the transformation process are classified into:

- natural resources
- semi-finished and finished goods
- services

These are respectively referred to as primary production, secondary production and tertiary production. Collectively, these three types of production (output) make up the three sectors that form the structure of industry:

- **Primary sector:** those organisations involved in extracting raw materials (e.g. farming, fishing, forestry and the extractive industries, such as oil exploration, mining and quarrying).
- **Secondary (manufacturing) sector:** those organisations involved in processing or refining the raw materials from the primary sector into finished or semi-finished products (e.g. paper mills, oil refineries, textile manufacturers, food processors, vehicle manufacturers and machine tools manufacturers).
- **Tertiary sector:** those organisations involved in providing services to customers and to other businesses, in either the public or the private sector (e.g. education, health, hairdressing, retailing, financial services, restaurants and leisure services).

Multiple outputs

Many transformation processes produce both goods and services. For example, a visit to a restaurant provides a service, but also leads to the production of a good from raw materials.

Production may also lead to undesirable outputs (e.g. pollution and waste) or unacceptable processes (e.g. the exploitation of child labour) as well as the goods and services produced. Increasingly, firms are being held responsible for these outputs through pressure groups, consumer action or government laws and regulations.

Feedback

The final part of the transformation model is feedback. Feedback of information is used to adapt the process in future to meet customer needs.

Adding value

Measuring output

How is output measured? This might seem to be an obvious question — surely if Toyota produces a car that is sold for £12,000, the value of its output is £12,000?

However, parts of this car (e.g. the radiator and tyres) may have been manufactured by another company and sold to Toyota as components. Therefore, the true value of this car is its selling price minus the value of goods and services bought in by Toyota. This is known as **value added**.

> **Key terms**
>
> **value added:** sales revenue minus the cost of bought-in materials, components and services.
> **adding value:** the process of increasing the worth of resources by modifying them.

The production process is seen to be a major factor in adding value. For example, the transformation of various components into a television set adds value, as people place a higher value on the television set than on the bits and pieces used to make it. Similarly, distribution and retailing add value by bringing the product within easier reach of the customer. Other services, such as marketing, also add value by:
- creating a unique selling point (USP) — this may be real, such as a different design or different components, or it may be based on image and branding
- identifying an attractive mix of design, function, image and service

> **Analysis**
>
> Opportunities for analysis are:
> - explaining why certain inputs or resources are used by a business
> - demonstrating how the transformation process adds value to resources
> - showing how a business can add value
> - analysing the benefits of adding value for a business

Evaluation

Opportunities for evaluation are:
- judging the choice of resources/inputs used by a business
- evaluating the suitability of the transformation process used by a start-up
- reasons why adding value is easier for some start-ups than others
- discussing the main factors that lead to a business adding value

Links

This topic links to the qualities of the entrepreneur — specifically their ability to decide on the best resources to use in order to produce a finished product that adds value. Adding value also depends on understanding the nature of the market and links closely to the relationship between costs and price, which is covered in financial planning.

Developing business plans

Key term

business plan: a report describing the marketing strategy, operational issues and financial implications of a business start-up.

Purpose of a business plan

Drawing up a business plan is an important step in setting up a new business. The key purposes and benefits of a business plan are:
- to help the entrepreneur to set clear objectives
- to guide the entrepreneur towards strategies or actions needed to meet these objectives
- to persuade lenders to invest capital in the business by demonstrating why it is likely to succeed — bank managers will want to see a business plan before giving bank loans or overdrafts
- to help in the running of the business by providing a working document against which the business's progress can be reviewed regularly
- to encourage entrepreneurs to plan ahead in a realistic way

Content of a business plan

The main sections of a business plan are:
- details about the business, including its name and location, the legal structure of the business and a description of the product or service
- personal information about the owner and those who will be managing the business, including their CVs and an account of their business skills, experience and financial commitments

- details about any support they are receiving, including mentors and other advisory agencies, and any training they have received or are undergoing
- details of key staff and staffing requirements
- the objectives of the firm or what it is aiming to achieve
- a marketing plan showing: the gap in the market that the business start-up is intended to fill; the results of any market research that has been done; the type, size and location of the market; a description of potential customers (e.g. age and gender); details of promotion and selling techniques to be used; and how the product will be priced
- a production plan detailing how goods and services will be created and the day-to-day practical details of the activities involved (the materials, staff and equipment needed, and capacity)
- details of fixed assets, such as premises and equipment
- sales and cash-flow forecast, and projected profit and loss account and balance sheet, for the next few years
- details of the finance needed from the lender or investor and the forecast speed of repayment or rate of return on the investor's capital
- the collateral (security) to be offered
- a brief account of the long-term forecasts and plans of the business
- a SWOT analysis that explains how the business intends to build on its strengths in order to exploit opportunities, and reduce its weaknesses in order to overcome any threats

Sources of information and guidance

There are many sources of information for a new business. These include:
- accountants — financial advice
- bank managers — financial advice
- Business Link — a government-funded service that provides general information, advice and support to start-ups
- local enterprise agencies
- chambers of commerce
- trade associations

(These three organisations above consist of local business people who help, advise and may provide useful contacts.)
- the Prince's Trust and PRIME, which offer help and funding for entrepreneurs aged 18–30 and those over 50 respectively

Analysis
Opportunities for analysis are:
- explaining the benefits of creating a business plan
- outlining the problems involved in business planning
- indicating how a good business plan can help competitive advantage

- analysing the relative merits of different sources of information used in developing a business plan
- demonstrating how the business plan might help the business succeed

Evaluation
Opportunities for evaluation are:
- the relative merits of different sources of information in constructing a sound business plan
- the importance of the business plan to the business
- evaluating the strengths and weaknesses of a particular business plan
- advising on how a business plan might be improved

Links
This topic provides an integrating theme for every topic in Unit 1. Virtually all of the topic areas in Unit 1 will be found in a business plan, and the skills of the entrepreneur in developing a good business plan will be a major influence on the potential success of the business start-up.

Conducting start-up market research

Key terms
marketing: the process of anticipating and satisfying customers' wants in a way that delights the customer and also meets the needs of the organisation.
market research: the systematic and objective collection, analysis and evaluation of information that is intended to assist the marketing process.

Purposes of market research
Market research is undertaken for descriptive, explanatory, predictive and exploratory reasons.

Descriptive reasons
The collection and analysis of data allows organisations to identify a number of important pieces of information. Examples are:
- Has the firm achieved its target sales figure?
- Are sales rising or falling? Is the trend stable or unpredictable?
- How are the firm's sales performing relative to a competitor?

Explanatory reasons
Market research can help an organisation to investigate why certain things occur. For example:
- What external factors affect demand?
- What are the main reasons why customers buy the product?
- Why was a promotional campaign unsuccessful?

Predictive reasons

Information can be used to predict trends and find links between sets of data. This will help the firm to predict what will happen in the future. Typical uses include:

- calculating the extent to which advertising influences sales volume
- discovering whether introducing a new flavour affects the sales of existing flavours
- predicting whether a new price will boost sales revenue

Exploratory reasons

For new start-ups there is often no existing market information to help an entrepreneur. Market research may help the enterprise to assess factors such as:

- the probable level of demand
- the most suitable market segments to be targeted
- the ideal price level
- the best ways of promoting the product

Types of market research

Market research is classified in two ways, according to:

- how the data are collected (primary or secondary)
- the content of the data (quantitative or qualitative)

How data are collected

There are two sources of information, **primary** and **secondary**.

> **Key terms**
>
> **primary market research:** the collection of information first-hand for a specific purpose.
> **secondary market research:** the use of information that has already been collected for a different purpose.

Primary market research

Researchers often go out (into the field) to collect primary data, so it is frequently called **field research**.

Methods of conducting primary research are described below.

Experiments

An organisation experiments with a particular approach in certain areas or for a certain time.

Benefits

- It is a relatively cheap way of finding out customer preferences.
- It considers actual customer behaviour rather than opinions given in a questionnaire.

Drawbacks

- Consumer behaviour may not be the same throughout the country.
- It may delay the introduction of a potentially successful strategy.

Observation

Stores watch customers while they are shopping and gather information on customer reactions.

Benefits
- The effectiveness of displays and merchandising can be assessed.
- It may show what customers are thinking.

Drawbacks
- It is expensive to employ psychologists to analyse the results.
- Observation shows what is happening rather than why it is taking place.

Focus groups

A group of consumers are encouraged to discuss their feelings about a product or market.

Benefits
- Focus groups enable a firm to gather in-depth details of consumers' thoughts.
- These groups also help to uncover new ideas on how to market products or services.

Drawbacks
- There may be a bias within a focus group.
- Focus groups are expensive to operate.

Surveys

Consumers are questioned about the product or service. Surveys can take a number of forms, but usually involve the completion of a questionnaire that is designed to collate the characteristics and views of a cross-section of consumers. The main types of survey are described below.

Personal interviews
These are conducted face-to-face, with the interviewer filling in the answers given by the interviewee.

Benefits
- A wide range of information can be gained.
- Any uncertainties in the wording of the question can be explained to the interviewee by the interviewer.

Drawbacks
- They can be time consuming.
- The interviewer may not select an unbiased sample or answers may not be truthful, if questions are personal.

Postal surveys
These surveys are posted to people who post them back after completion.

Benefits
- This method is cheap.
- Postal surveys allow more specific targeting of geographical areas.

- Respondents have more time to answer the questions, so much more detail can be put into the survey.

Drawbacks

- Response rates are usually low (often less than 2% are returned if no incentive is given).
- Returns may be biased, as people completing them may have a strong opinion.

Telephone interviews

These interviews take place when a market researcher telephones a member of the public, seeking their answers to certain questions.

Benefits

- Telephone calls are cheap and can be targeted directly at known customers.
- They are also used because they 'get entry into the house'.

Drawbacks

- Questions tend to be brief, as interviewees are reluctant to give too much time on the telephone.
- The increased use of unpopular telesales (often initially disguised as a survey) has led to customer resentment of any companies trying to contact members of the public at home.

Internet surveys

Questionnaires on internet sites enable customers to express their views about a product, service or company.

Benefits

- It is relatively inexpensive to place a questionnaire on a website.
- Internet surveys tend to target those most likely to be interested in buying the product, as they have made a conscious decision to visit the website.
- The surveys can be updated quite frequently, giving the business excellent topical data.
- It may be possible to provide quite detailed questionnaires, particularly if an incentive is provided to the respondent.

Drawbacks

- The sample will tend to be biased towards people with a particular interest in the product or service.
- It will be less relevant for organisations whose target market is non-internet users.

Test marketing

By launching a product in a limited part of a market, usually a geographical area, a firm can discover customer opinions.

Benefits

- The results of test marketing are a relatively accurate predictor of future popularity.
- Test marketing is a useful way of gauging the popularity of the product without incurring the huge expense of a national launch.

Drawbacks

- Fewer firms now employ the technique because it can lead to 'me-too' products (copies) being produced by rivals before the national launch.
- In rapidly changing markets, the delay in launching a product nationally may endanger the chances of making a profit from a new launch.

Secondary market research

Secondary information is found by examining published documents (i.e. through **desk research**).

Secondary research data can take many forms. Firms will select data that suit their particular purposes. Some key sources are:

- government publications
- newspapers
- company records
- magazines
- competitors
- market research organisations
- loyalty cards
- the internet

Benefits of secondary market research

- The information is already available, so quick decisions can be taken based upon it.
- It is cheaper than primary research.
- Secondary surveys are often conducted regularly, so the information obtained is particularly helpful in identifying trends over time.

Drawbacks of secondary market research

- The information may be dated, and therefore could be misleading.
- The data are available to other firms, so it is less likely that the data will give the organisation any advantages over its competitors.
- There may be no relevant secondary data to meet the specific needs of the firm.
- The data are collected by other organisations for their own use, so the secondary user may not know their level of accuracy and reliability.

Content of the data

The content of information obtained by market research can be **qualitative** or **quantitative**.

> **Key terms**
>
> **qualitative market research:** the collection of information about the market based on subjective factors such as opinions and reasons.
>
> **quantitative market research:** the collection of information about the market based on numbers.

Qualitative market research

Qualitative research deals with issues such as: why and how?

Benefits of qualitative market research

- A business can gain a greater insight into what it needs to do to appeal to its consumers.
- This research can provide ideas that the firm was not aware of, so it can take action to overcome problems or seize opportunities that it might not have considered beforehand.
- Qualitative research can give detailed insights into customers' thinking when they buy a product, and a firm can modify its marketing strategies accordingly

Problems of qualitative market research

- It is expensive to gather, as it usually requires skilled personnel to interpret it.
- Consequently, most qualitative research is conducted on a small scale. This can lead to bias or unrepresentative opinions, if the sample is inappropriate.
- It is difficult to tabulate and compare with other data, as the opinions are often unstructured.

Quantitative market research

Quantitative research can answer the following questions: how many, who and how often?

Benefits of quantitative market research

- It summarises data in a concise and meaningful way.
- The use of numerical data makes it easier to compare results with other organisations.
- Numerical data can be used to identify trends and project future trends.

Problems of quantitative market research

- It only shows 'what', rather than explaining 'why'.
- It can lack reliability and validity if the sample is biased or too small.

Sampling

Primary market research is undertaken by sampling the views of a small selection of consumers. When conducting market research, firms will try to get a reasonably large **sample** so that their results are reliable.

> **Key term**
>
> **sample:** a group of respondents or factors whose views or behaviour should be representative of the target market as a whole.

The **sample size** measures the number of people or items in the sample. When conducting primary research, a firm needs to balance the need for accuracy against the cost of the survey. Large samples increase reliability but cost more. Small samples decrease costs but are less reliable.

random sample: a group of respondents in which each member of the target population has an equal chance of being chosen.

quota sample: a group of respondents comprising several different segments, each sharing a common feature (e.g. age, gender). The number of interviewees in each classification is fixed to reflect their percentage in the total target population, but the interviewees are selected non-randomly by the interviewer.

stratified sample: a group of respondents selected according to particular features (e.g. age, gender). However, unlike quota sampling, where the final selection is left to an interviewer, in stratified sampling the subgroups and their sizes are chosen specifically.

The general problems of sampling are as follows:
- Samples may be unrepresentative (e.g. asking the wrong people).
- There may be bias in questions or in the answers that they encourage.
- It may be difficult to locate suitable respondents (e.g. people who listen to a particular radio programme).

Factors influencing the choice of sampling method
The choice of sampling method is affected by the following factors:
- **Costs and the availability of finance.** Random sampling is cheaper because it does not involve careful planning of the sample before the survey is conducted.
- **Time.** If quick results are needed, a random sample or a quota sample can be surveyed much more speedily.
- **The importance of market segments/sections.** If buying behaviour is very different between different types of consumer, quota or stratified sampling will be necessary to examine the different patterns of behaviour of the different sections or segments of the market.
- **Is the business targeting a specific group of customers?** If market research is endeavouring to identify the opinions of just one target group, it is essential that quota or stratified sampling is used, so that only this target group is surveyed.
- **The firm's understanding of its customer base.** If the firm is unaware of the types of customer that it will attract (or attracts), there will be no point in using quota or stratified sampling — they both depend on a prior understanding of the types of customer.

Opportunities for analysis are:
- outlining the purposes of market research
- explaining the benefits/problems of primary/secondary market research
- explaining the benefits/problems of qualitative/quantitative market research
- recognising the factors that influence the size and/or type of sample used by a business
- comparing the relative merits of random, quota and stratified sampling
- analysing the factors that influence the choice of sampling method and size of sample

Opportunities for evaluation are:

- the relative merits of different forms of market research, such as primary v. secondary and qualitative v. quantitative
- an overall assessment of the quality of market research conducted by a new entrepreneur
- judgement of the strengths and weaknesses of the sampling methods chosen in a new business start-up

This topic links closely to the development of the business idea, as market research is needed to identify the product and the market niche targeted. Market research is essential, as it enables a business to understand its market. It may also link to location, as the market is one of the factors influencing the location of a business. Thorough and accurate market research can reduce the risk of a business start-up by providing a good understanding of the business world.

Understanding markets

market: a place where buyers and sellers come together.

The nature and types of market

Markets can be classified in different ways.

Geographical classification

This classification is based on the geographical area targeted by business organisations:

- local markets (e.g. a plumber)
- national markets (e.g. Nationwide Building Society)

Physical and non-physical markets

This classification is based on the way in which products are bought and sold.

- **Physical markets.** In a physical market there is an actual place where buyers and sellers meet.
- **Electronic/non-physical markets.** For many goods and services, the traditional, physical market is being replaced by marketplaces that take advantage of the opportunities presented by modern technology, selling via the telephone or internet.

Other classifications of markets

- Markets can be classified according to the type of customer. This is known as **market segmentation**.

- Markets may also be classified according to the level of competition in the market.

Importance of demand

Demand is the amount of a product or service that consumers are willing and able to buy at any given price over a period of time.

Factors influencing the demand for a product

Demand for a product is determined by the following factors:

- **Price.** As the price of a product rises, the demand for it will usually fall, and vice versa. However, products such as necessities may be bought in similar quantities whatever the price charged.
- **Income and wealth.** As consumers' incomes increase, their overall demand for products will increase. Furthermore, the pattern of their demand will change — they will purchase more luxuries but fewer basic goods.
- **Tastes and fashion.** Over time people's tastes and fashions change. Such changes will affect the demand for products and services.
- **Prices of other goods.** Sometimes the demand for a product can be influenced by the price of a totally different product. This occurs in two instances — when the products are either substitutes or complements.
- **Demographic factors.** Demographic factors are those related to population. The UK population has grown in recent years and this has led to an overall increase in demand. Within this increase there have been changes in the geographical spread of the population, its ethnic balance, the size of households and the age distribution of the population. These changes have also led to changes in the types of product demanded.
- **Marketing and advertising.** Successful marketing and promotion can have a major impact upon the demand for a good or service.
- **Government action.** Government can influence the demand for a product by subsidising it, taxing it and using its own advertising campaigns either to encourage or discourage the purchase of a product.

Types of market segmentation

Key term

market segmentation: the classification of customers or potential customers into groups or subgroups (market segments), each of which responds differently to different products or marketing approaches.

Markets can be segmented in the following ways:

- **Age.** For many products and services, age is a crucial influence on demand, so firms will segment on this basis.
- **Gender (sex).** Some products are targeted specifically at males or females.
- **Social class.** In general, social class influences purchasing habits because class A will receive more income than class B and so on.

- **Residential.** For example, ACORN (A Classification Of Residential Neighbourhoods) segments the market according to types of housing. Families in suburban detached houses are expected to have very different tastes from those living in terraced houses in rural areas.
- **Geographic.** Although regional variations in taste are becoming less significant, there are still major differences in tastes and purchasing behaviour based on geographical features.

Note: businesses will identify and target the market segment or segments that are relevant to their products and services.

Benefits of market segmentation

Market segmentation can help a firm:

- to increase market share
- to develop new products
- to extend products into new markets
- to identify ways of marketing a product

Drawbacks of market segmentation

Market segmentation may involve the following problems:

- difficulty in identifying the most important segments for a product
- not knowing how to reach the chosen segment with the firm's marketing
- being unable to keep up-to-date with the changing views of the target market segment
- potential for ignoring other market segments

Market size, growth and share

> **Key terms**
>
> **market size:** the volume of sales of a product (e.g. the number of computers sold) or the value of sales of a product (e.g. the total revenue from computer sales).
> **market growth:** the percentage change in sales (volume or value) over a period of time.

Factors influencing market growth

A business should be aware of the factors that influence growth, so that it can predict future trends. Key factors are as follows:

- **Economic growth.** If a country's wealth is growing by 3% per annum, sales are likely to rise in any given market.
- **The nature of the product.** Markets for luxury products tend to be more volatile.
- **Changes in taste and fashion.** As lifestyles change, new products become more popular while others decline.
- **Social changes.** The way in which people live may influence product sales.

> **Key term**
>
> **market share:** the percentage or proportion of the total sales of a product or service achieved by a firm or a specific brand of a product.

Market share is usually measured as a percentage, calculated by the formula:

$$\text{market share} = \frac{\text{sales of one product or brand or company}}{\text{total sales in the market}} \times 100$$

Market share is an excellent measure of a company's success because it compares a firm's sales with those of its competitors. A company's market share can increase only if the company is performing better than some of its rivals.

Analysis

Opportunities for analysis are:
- indicating the reasons why the business has targeted a particular type of market
- explaining the factors that influence the demand for a particular product
- analysing the benefits and/or drawbacks of specific types of market segmentation for a particular business
- assessing the benefits and problems of market segmentation in general to a business
- analysing the impact of market size, growth or share on a business

Evaluation

Opportunities for evaluation are:
- assessing the type of market that a business should target
- the relative importance of different factors that influence the demand for the business's products or services
- weighing up the benefits and problems involved in using market segmentation
- deciding on which market segment(s) to target
- deciding how to target given market segment(s)

Links

This topic links closely to the development of the business idea, as the success of an idea is dependent on the qualities of the product and the market niche targeted. It also relates to market research, which is needed to help the business to understand its market. It may also link to 'location', as the market is one of the factors influencing the location of a business. A good understanding of the market can reduce the risk facing a business start-up.

Choosing the right legal structure for the business

Types of legal structure

The types of legal structure in the private sector are as follows:

Unincorporated businesses
- sole trader
- partnership

Incorporated businesses
- private limited company
- public limited company

Unincorporated and incorporated businesses

> **Key terms**
>
> **unincorporated business:** a firm in which there is no distinction in law between the individual owner and the business itself. The identity of the business and the owner is the same. Such businesses tend to be sole traders or partnerships.
>
> **incorporated business:** a firm with a legal identity that is separate from the individual owners. Such organisations can own assets, owe money and enter into contracts in their own right. They include private limited companies and public limited companies.

Unlimited liability and limited liability

> **Key terms**
>
> **unlimited liability:** a situation in which the owners of a business are liable for all the debts that the business may incur.
>
> **limited liability:** a situation in which the liability of the owners of a business is limited to the fully paid-up value of the share capital.

Sole trader

A sole trader is a business owned by one person, but the owner may employ other people.

Features
- Sole traders usually have little capital for expansion.
- No protection is offered against debts as sole traders have unlimited liability.
- Sole traders are often found in the provision of local services: for example, your local newsagent, plumber and hairdresser are likely to be sole traders.

Advantages
- Sole traders are easy and cheap to set up.
- There are few legal formalities.
- They are able to respond quickly to changes in circumstances.
- The owner takes all of the profit and hence there is good motivation.
- They have greater independence than other legal structures.
- They enjoy more privacy, as their financial details do not have to be published.

Disadvantages
- Sole traders have unlimited liability.
- They have limited collateral to support applications for loans.
- They have limited capital for investment and expansion.
- There are difficulties when the owner wishes to go on holiday or is ill.
- They have limited skills, as the owner needs to be a 'jack of all trades'.

THE HENLEY COLLEGE LIBRARY

content guidance

Partnership

A partnership is a form of business in which two or more people operate for the common goal of making a profit.

Features

- Partners usually have unlimited liability, although it is possible for partners to have limited liability in some circumstances.
- A partnership agreement usually sets down the rights and responsibilities of the members of the partnership and how profits will be allocated.
- In the absence of an agreement, profits are shared equally among all partners.
- A partnership has potential for more capital than a sole trader.
- Decisions and responsibilities are shared.

Advantages

- Between them, partners may have a wide range of skills and knowledge.
- Partners are able to raise greater amounts of capital than sole traders.
- The pressure on owners is reduced, as cover is available for holidays, and decisions are made jointly.

Disadvantages

- Control is shared among the partners.
- Arguments are common among partners.
- There is still an absolute shortage of capital — even 20 people can only raise so much.
- Partnerships have unlimited liability (unless a limited liability partnership has been established).

Private limited company

A private limited company is a small to medium-sized business that is usually run by the family or the small group of individuals who own it.

Features

- A private limited company can keep its affairs reasonably private.
- Private companies are funded by shares that cannot be sold without the agreement of the other shareholders.
- The share capital of private companies may be less then £50,000, although many have much higher levels of share capital.
- Private limited companies generally tend to be limited in size.
- A private limited company must have 'Ltd' after the company name to warn people that its owners (shareholders) have limited liability.

Advantages

- A private company has limited liability and a legal identity separate from its owners.
- It has access to more capital than unincorporated businesses.
- It enjoys more privacy than a public limited company (plc), as it is only required to divulge a limited amount of financial information and as a result is subject to less pressure from outside investors.

- It is more flexible than a plc.

Disadvantages
- Its shares are less attractive, as they cannot be traded on the Stock Exchange and hence could be difficult to sell.
- It is less flexible if expansion needs finance, which is more difficult to raise than for a plc.
- There are more legal formalities than for an unincorporated business.

Public limited company

A public limited company (plc) is a business with limited liability, a share capital of over £50,000, at least two shareholders, two directors and a qualified company secretary, and usually a wide spread of shareholders.

Features
- Shares can be traded on the Stock Exchange.
- Therefore it is usually easier for these businesses to raise finance.
- Control changes from a close-knit group of individuals towards a much broader scrutiny of the firm's affairs.
- A public limited company must have 'plc' after the company name.

Advantages
- The business has limited liability and a legal identity separate from its owners.
- It is easier to raise finance as a result of its Stock Exchange listing.
- It has greater scope for new investment.
- It can gain positive publicity as a result of trading on the Stock Exchange.
- Suppliers tend to be more willing to offer credit to public limited companies.

Disadvantages
- It has to publish a great deal of financial information about its performance.
- There is greater scrutiny of its activities.
- It has significant administrative expenses.
- The founders of the firm may lose control if their shareholding falls below 50%.
- A Stock Exchange listing means that pressure from investors may lead to more emphasis on short-term financial results rather than long-term performance.

Not-for-profit organisations

Not-for-profit organisations aim to break even financially. The sector includes voluntary and community organisations, charities, social enterprises, pressure groups, cooperatives, mutual societies and trusts. There are an estimated 400,000 not-for-profit organisations, of which approximately 180,000 are charities registered with the Charity Commission.

Features
Although the organisations vary, they share the following common characteristics:
- They are non-governmental organisations.
- They have a governing body responsible for managing their affairs.

- They are value-driven and have social, environmental, community, welfare or cultural aims and objectives.
- They are usually established for purposes other than financial gain, with any profits or surpluses being reinvested in the organisation in order to further its objectives.
- Many use volunteer staff in addition to paid employees.

Thus although these organisations may make profit, their objective is not to maximise profit for their shareholders and owners. Instead their main objectives are based on providing services to customers, employees or other groups.

Analysis

Opportunities for analysis are:
- assessing the benefits and drawbacks of the sole trader as the legal structure for a business
- carrying out a similar analysis for partnerships and private limited companies
- explaining the reasons for a business wanting to have limited liability
- comparing the relative merits of two different forms of legal structure, such as sole trader v. partnership
- conveying the reasons why some businesses choose to operate on a not-for-profit basis

Evaluation

Opportunities for evaluation are:
- the significance of limited liability for a business
- discussion of the relative merits of different forms of legal structure for a business in a particular situation
- issues involved in deciding whether a business should change its legal status
- the implications of being a not-for-profit business

Links

The choice of legal structure is an essential element of any business plan and it relates to the wishes of the entrepreneur, such as independence or a desire to work with others. The choice of legal structure also affects the way in which finance is raised.

Raising finance

The main sources of finance for a start-up business include the following:
- ordinary share capital
- venture capital
- loan capital (e.g. bank loans)
- bank overdrafts
- personal sources

Ordinary share capital

Ordinary share capital is money given to a company by shareholders in return for a share certificate. This gives them part ownership of the company and entitles them to a share of the profits.

Because ordinary shareholders are usually given one vote for each share, ownership of 51% of the shares in a company guarantees overall control of that company.

Advantages of ordinary share capital
- Limited liability encourages shareholders to invest in the business, as it restricts the amount of money they can lose.
- It is not necessary to pay shareholders a dividend if the business cannot afford these payments.
- Bringing new shareholders into a small business can often mean that further expertise is brought into the business.
- Increasing ordinary share capital can make it easier to borrow more funds from a bank, as the share capital can purchase assets that can be used as collateral.
- Ordinary share capital does not need to be repaid, so it eases the pressure on a limited company.

Disadvantages of ordinary share capital
- In profitable years, ordinary shareholders will expect good dividends and this is likely to be more expensive than the interest charged on a loan.
- The original aims of the business may be lost, as new shareholders may not have the same values as the original owners.
- As more shares are sold to raise finance, the original owners may lose control of the business.

Loan capital

Loan capital is money received by an organisation in return for the organisation's agreement to pay interest during the period of the loan and to repay the loan within an agreed time.

A **bank loan** is a sum of money provided to a firm or an individual by a bank for a specific, agreed purpose.

Advantages of bank loans
- The interest rate and thus the repayments are fixed in advance, making it easy to budget the schedule for repayments.
- Interest rates are normally lower because of the security provided.
- The size of the loan and the period of repayment can be organised to match the exact needs of the firm.

Disadvantages of bank loans
- The size of the loan may be limited by the amount of collateral that can be provided rather than by the amount of money needed by the business.

- It is often difficult or costly to repay a loan early.
- Start-ups are often charged higher rates of interest because they are unable to provide the guarantees that the bank manager might like.

Bank overdrafts

A bank overdraft is when a bank allows an organisation to overspend its current account at the bank up to an agreed (overdraft) limit and for a stated time period.

Advantages of bank overdrafts
- They are extremely flexible and useful for temporary cash-flow problems.
- Interest is only paid on the amount of the overdraft being used.
- They are particularly useful to seasonal businesses, which are likely to experience some cash-flow problems at certain times of the year.
- Security is not usually required.

Disadvantages of bank overdrafts
- The interest rate charged is usually higher than for a loan.
- Banks can demand immediate repayment (although this is rare).

Venture capital

Venture capital is finance that is provided to small or medium-sized firms that seek growth, but which may be considered as risky by typical share buyers or other lenders.

Advantages of venture capital
- Venture capital is available to firms that are unable to get finance from other sources because of the risk involved.
- Venture capitalists sometimes allow interest or dividends to be delayed.
- Venture capitalists may provide advice and guidance.

Disadvantages of venture capital
- Venture capitalists often want a significant share of the business in return.
- Venture capitalists often want high interest payments or dividends.
- It is possible that venture capitalists will exert too much influence, so the original owner may lose their independence.

Personal sources

This is money that is provided by the owner or owners of the business from their own savings or personal wealth. The advantages and disadvantages of the main sources of personal finance are listed below.

Personal savings
Advantages
- This is a cheap source.
- It enables the owners to keep control of the business.

Disadvantages
- A person can quickly lose their savings.
- The entrepreneurs may not have sufficient savings to finance a new business.

Mortgage
Advantages
- A second mortgage may enable a homeowner to raise a substantial sum of money.
- The interest rates charged on mortgages tend to be lower than on other loans.

Disadvantages
- If the business is unsuccessful, the owner may lose their property.
- Many entrepreneurs will not own a sufficiently valuable property.

Private borrowing from friends and family
Advantages
- Friends and family may be prepared to lend money when the bank would refuse.
- Friends and family often provide easier repayment terms.
- The additional money raised through friends and family may encourage a bank manager to offer a further loan.

Disadvantages
- Owing money to friends and family can increase stress.
- It can undermine friendships, as there may be disputes about when and how much money should be repaid.

Selling private assets
Advantages
- This may mean that an asset that was previously of no real use to a person is used productively.
- It is possible that the asset can be leased back by the owner and still used.

Disadvantages
- This can cause family tensions, as the business may be seen to be benefiting at the expense of the family.
- It is unlikely that large sums of money can be raised by selling off private assets.

Classification of sources of finance by time period

Long-term finance	Medium-term finance	Short-term finance
Personal sources	Personal sources	Personal sources
Ordinary share capital		
Loan capital/bank loan	Loan capital/bank loan	
		Bank overdraft
Venture capital	Venture capital	

Which source of finance should be chosen?

When deciding which source of finance to use, a business person will weigh up the following factors:

- **Legal structure of the business.** Private limited companies (Ltds) and public limited companies (plcs) will sell shares; sole traders and partnerships will rely on personal finance.
- **Use of the finance.** The basic rule is that the length of time that it takes the business to earn the money needed to repay the source should match the length of time the business is given to repay the money.
- **Amount required.** More than one source may be needed.
- **Level of risk.** If an enterprise is viewed as risky, firms will find it harder to attract loans, although venture capital may be a possibility.
- **Views of the owners.** Shareholders or owners may be reluctant to lose control of a firm, so they may reject shares and venture capital.

Analysis

Opportunities for analysis are:

- analysing the advantages of a specific form of finance in a certain context
- showing the disadvantages of a certain form of finance in a given context
- analysis of situations in which more than one source of finance is needed
- examining the link between the source of finance and the timescale needed for repayment
- linking the appropriateness of a given method of raising finance to the financial background of the start-up

Evaluation

Opportunities for evaluation are:

- assessing the pros and cons of different sources of finance for a start-up business
- appreciating the need to modify a business's method of raising finance in the light of changing circumstances
- evaluating the main factors involved in deciding the most suitable form of finance for a particular need

Links

The ability to raise finance is a central issue in a business start-up. In this respect it links in with every other element of Unit 1. The level of risk, whether a business idea can be protected, whether a business can afford to buy a franchise, how much market research it can afford — these are all linked back to this one factor. When analysing any other area of the specification in which a decision involves the expenditure of money, it is worth considering whether and how the business can raise the necessary finance.

Locating the business

Business decisions concerning location are influenced by a range of factors.

Technology

Technology is becoming an increasingly important influence on location decisions for start-ups because of **teleworking**. Teleworking involves working in a location that is separate from a central workplace, using telecommunication technologies. There are currently 3.3 million teleworkers, 62% of them self-employed.

Many start-ups operate from home because of:
- flexibility as telecommunications allow a person to stay in contact while travelling
- cost/lack of overheads
- time flexibility, enabling staff to work outside normal office hours

Technology is also a factor in the location of small manufacturing businesses. If technological equipment is needed, it is very unlikely that a small business will be able to operate from the home of the owner.

Costs of factors of production

The main assumption made about location decisions is that firms will locate at the least-cost site. This is the business location that allows a firm to minimise its costs (and hence its selling price).

For start-ups and small businesses, it is vital that costs are kept to a minimum in order to give the business a chance to compete with larger competitors.

The main costs influencing the location of businesses are:
- **Land costs/rent.** This is important for small firms because land costs potentially represent such a large percentage of total costs.
- **Labour costs.** In the UK there are significant variations in wage levels between regions. However, a highly skilled and efficient labour force may compensate for slightly higher wage levels through greater labour productivity and higher quality.
- **Transport costs.** These are important for both raw materials and finished goods.
- **Suppliers.** The location of suppliers may be a factor influencing business location, especially if speed of delivery is important.

Infrastructure

Infrastructure is a network of utilities, such as transport links, sewerage, telecommunications systems, health services and educational facilities.

For small businesses, the local infrastructure may be more important than the regional or national infrastructure. The following questions are particularly significant to a small business:
- Are parking spaces available nearby?

- How much does it cost to park?
- Is traffic flow good?
- Is it on a bus route or close to a station?
- If the business is a shop, is it isolated or convenient for visits to other shops?
- Is it easy to receive deliveries?

The market

For retailers and other service industries, the market is often the most important influence on location. As the UK's economy is predominantly based on tertiary production (the provision of services), this makes the market a crucial factor in determining the location of many UK firms.

In deciding on location, small retailers will look at the **footfall** in an area (the number of potential customers walking past the shop). These firms will also research the types of customer to see whether they are likely to be interested in their products. Organisations such as estate agents and charity shops often locate close to each other so that potential customers will be drawn to the area by competitors and are then likely to visit their premises.

Qualitative factors

Ultimately, all business decisions are taken by individuals, often without access to perfect forecasts of the implications of the different choices available. Consequently, directors may base their choices on factors other than business criteria. Examples are:
- where the entrepreneur lives
- the prestige of an area
- local facilities in an area
- quality of life in an area

Government intervention

The government gives grants (gifts) to firms in Assisted Areas — parts of England that have relatively low levels of economic activity and high and persistent unemployment.

Locating small businesses

Research has shown that the key factors influencing small business locations are:
- demographic factors, such as whether the local population matches the target market
- the economic wealth of the local area and whether it can support the number of businesses located in the vicinity
- pedestrian traffic flow (footfall) during opening times
- parking factors — cost and time
- competitors' locations — is competition fierce or will it attract potential customers into the area?

- location history — does the individual site have a good track record of successful business activity?
- council policies, such as limiting certain business activities (e.g. nightclubs) to certain areas of a town

Analysis

Opportunities for analysis are:
- analysing the factors that influence the start-up location
- comparing the relative merits of alternative locations
- recognising that the relative importance of a factor may vary according to the type of business

Note that location decisions can not only be analysed through interpretation of passages of text, but may also be based on numerical/financial data or maps.

Evaluation

Opportunities for evaluation are:
- recognising the relative importance of different factors influencing start-up location decisions
- judging the relative importance of qualitative factors in a location decision
- assessing whether changes in circumstances necessitate a change in location

Links

Location decisions are a central part of the business plan. They may be influenced by government support for entrepreneurs and also link closely to the market and target market segments. Location decisions are heavily based on financial factors such as costs and the potential to generate revenue.

Employing people

Reasons for employing people

Entrepreneurs setting up a new business will need to employ people for a number of reasons:
- Only in the smallest businesses will the owner have the capacity to carry out all the tasks needed to provide the finished product or service.
- An entrepreneur will not often have all the skills required to run a business, and so will need to employ people with certain expertise.
- Some businesses are seasonal in nature and will need to employ more staff at peak times.

Types of employee used in small businesses
- **Permanent employees** (who may be full time or part time) have a continuous employment contract with the business.

- **Temporary employees** have a fixed-term employment contract, so their employment ends at a certain time (or after certain work has been completed).
- **Zero-hours contracts** allow a business to have people on-call to work whenever necessary and mutually convenient.
- **Agency staff** have contracts with an employment agency. A firm hires them for an agreed time from the employment agency.
- **Self-employed freelancers, consultants and contractors** offer their skills to a business for an agreed sum, but work for themselves.

Permanent or temporary staff?

Permanent staff are those needed throughout the year and whose services are necessary to the continued running of the business. They tend to be more motivated than temporary staff, who have less loyalty to the business.

Temporary staff are those needed to meet seasonal demand, to complete a particular task or to cover for situations such as staff illness and holidays.

Full-time or part-time staff?

Advantages of full-time workers
- Full-time workers are available for more hours.
- They are likely to be more loyal than part-timers.
- Full-time employment is a more popular option for most workers, so a firm may find it easier to recruit full-time employees.
- It is cheaper to recruit, train and administer one full-time member of staff than a number of part-time staff.

Advantages of part-time workers
- They keep costs down in areas where full-time cover is not necessary.
- They give flexibility, allowing a business to respond to changes in demand by changing the hours worked.
- The availability of part-time work may suit certain workers. Consequently the opportunity to work part time may mean that the business is able to retain valued employees.

External consultants, contractors and advisers

In addition to employees, a business might hire the services of consultants, contractors and advisers. As these people will be self-employed or belong to a separate company, this is a useful way of taking advantage of extra skills and labour without incurring unnecessary costs.

Drawbacks and difficulties of employing people

Drawbacks include the following:

- **Cost of employing people.** As well as the actual wage or salary paid, businesses incur other costs such as national insurance contributions, possible pension contributions and extensive administrative costs.
- **Meeting the range of employment legislation requirements.** This is often a burden for small businesses, as they lack specialist knowledge of employment laws.
- **Managing staff.** An entrepreneur in a start-up business may not have the skills to manage employees.
- **Employee absence.** This can be a major problem in a very small firm because it is difficult to cover absences.

Analysis

Opportunities for analysis are:

- analysing the reasons why a small business might employ staff
- comparing the relative merits of temporary and permanent staff
- comparing the relative merits of full-time and part-time staff
- demonstrating the need for a blend of temporary and permanent or full-time and part-time staff
- showing the drawbacks and difficulties of employing people
- recognising situations in which the use of consultants and advisers is necessary
- examining the problems involved in employing consultants and advisers

Evaluation

Opportunities for evaluation are:

- appreciating the relative merits of full-time and part-time or temporary and permanent employees in different situations
- evaluating situations in which the use of consultants and advisers is particularly useful
- discussing the main difficulties for a particular business arising from its employment of people

Links

This topic links to the legal structure of the business, as limited companies are likely to employ far more people. There may be links to the impact of employing people on the objectives of the entrepreneur. Employing people also has major financial implications for a business.

Financial planning
Calculating costs, revenues and profits

Price, total revenue and profit

Key terms

price: the amount paid by a consumer to purchase 1 unit of a product.
total revenue: a measure of the income received from an organisation's activities.
Total revenue = price per unit × quantity of units sold (e.g. if price is £12 and 6 units
are sold, total revenue is £12 × 6 = £72).
profit: the difference between the income of a business and its total costs. Profit =
total revenue − total costs.

Price
A business must set a price that is:
- high enough to cover the costs of making the product
- low enough to attract customers

The ideal selling price is the one that helps the firm to make the most profit (or helps
to achieve other aims of the business).

Total revenue
Total revenue may also be described by the following terms:
- income
- revenue
- sales revenue
- sales turnover
- turnover

Profit
Making a profit is a prime objective of most firms. In effect, there are two ways of
improving profit:
- increasing sales revenue
- decreasing costs

A combination of both is the ideal way of achieving additional profit.

Costs
Some functional areas of a business, such as production and administration, can help
to achieve rising profits by reducing costs, but the business must be careful that these
cost savings are not reducing the quality of the good or service.

Key terms

fixed costs: costs that do not vary directly with output in the short run (e.g. rent).
variable costs: costs that vary directly with output in the short run (e.g. raw materials).
total costs: the sum of fixed costs and variable costs.

If there is a 20% rise in output, it is assumed that:

- fixed costs do not change
- variable costs change by the same percentage as the change in output (20% in this case)

This is an oversimplification of what actually happens in real life, but it is helpful to firms because it allows them to make fairly accurate predictions about how costs will change as output changes. In turn, this will assist them in making logical business decisions.

Classification of some typical costs

Fixed costs	Variable costs
Machinery	Raw materials
Rent and rates	Wages of operatives/direct labour
Salaries	Power
Administration	
Vehicles	
Marketing	
Lighting and heating	

Effect of changes in output on costs

Total units of output (000s)	Fixed costs (£000s)	Variable costs (£000s)	Total costs (£000s)
0	80	0	80
10	80	40	120
20	80	80	160
30	80	120	200
40	80	160	240
50	80	200	280
60	80	240	320

Annual costs and output for product X

Note how total costs are rising at a slower rate than output because only the variable costs are increasing as output increases.

Relationship between costs and price

In many industries, increases in costs (e.g. for raw materials and labour) are 'passed on' to the consumer in the form of higher prices. Although business theory suggests that higher prices will lead to a fall in demand (and possibly in sales revenue), demand is less likely to fall if every business is increasing its prices. This is likely to happen when costs are increasing, because all firms will be affected in a similar way and they will all be trying to maintain a **profit margin** (the difference between the selling price of an item and the cost of making or buying that item).

Analysis

Opportunities for analysis are:
- understanding the relationship between costs, price, revenue and profits
- assessing the impact of a change in one of these variables on the performance of the business
- advising the entrepreneur on changes in price and cost, and their impact on the business

Evaluation

Opportunities for evaluation are:
- interpretation of the extent to which changes in costs and/or revenue can impact upon profit
- recognition of situations in which changes in profit arising from changes in output can be greatly influenced by the balance of fixed and variable costs
- assessing the relative significance of price changes for sales revenue and/or profit

Links

The topics in all sections of Unit 1 have financial repercussions which will affect costs and revenue. Consequently, this section is a vital integrating link throughout Unit 1. It links most closely with the remainder of financial planning, particularly breakeven analysis. It is also likely that a major objective of a business is to make a profit. Thus this section will be vital in assessing the success or failure of a business start-up.

Using breakeven analysis to make decisions

Contribution

Key term

contribution per unit: selling price per unit − variable cost per unit.

For example, if the variable costs of making a candle are 15p and the candle sells for 38p, the contribution per unit is 23p (38p − 15p).

Key term

total contribution: the difference between sales revenue and total variable costs.

If total contribution is greater than fixed costs, the business makes a profit.

If total contribution is less than fixed costs, the business makes a loss.

The total contribution of a product can be calculated in two ways:
- total contribution = contribution per unit × no. of units sold
- total contribution = sales revenue – total variable costs

Calculating contribution per unit and total contribution

fixed costs (per year): £9,000
variable costs: £1.10 per unit
selling price (per unit): £2.60
no. of units sold (per year): 14,000
contribution per unit = £2.60 – £1.10 = £1.50

Using the first of the two formulae above:

total contribution = £1.50 × 14,000 = £21,000

Using the second formula:

(14,000 × £2.60) – (14,000 × £1.10) = £36,400 – £15,400 = £21,000
annual profit = total contribution – fixed costs = £21,000 – £9,000 = £12,000

Breakeven

Key terms

breakeven output: the level of output at which total sales revenue is equal to total costs of production.
breakeven analysis: study of the relationship between total costs and total revenue to identify the output at which a business breaks even (i.e. makes neither a profit nor a loss).

Assumptions of breakeven analysis

Breakeven analysis makes the following assumptions:
- The selling price per unit stays the same, regardless of the number of units sold.
- Fixed costs remain the same, regardless of the number of units of output.
- Variable costs per unit stay the same, regardless of output.
- Every unit of output that is produced is sold.

Calculating breakeven output
Using a formula

$$\text{breakeven output} = \frac{\text{fixed costs (£)}}{\text{contribution per unit (£)}}$$

Applying the data from earlier:

$$\text{breakeven output} = \frac{£9,000}{£2.60 - £1.10} = \frac{£9,000}{£1.50} = 6,000 \text{ units}$$

Using a graph

The graph shows the breakeven chart for a product based on the following data:

    fixed costs (FC_1) = £30,000

    variable costs per unit (VC_1) = £5

    selling price = £12.50 per unit

The breakeven point is shown on the graph. Breakeven output is 4,000 units.

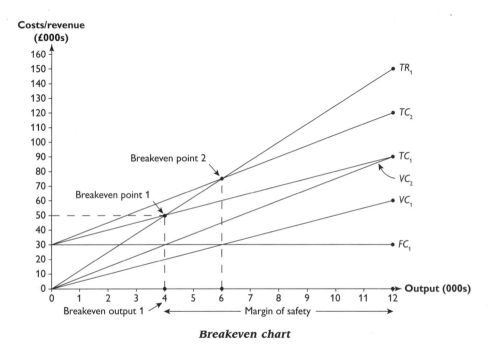

Breakeven chart

If variable costs per unit rise to £7.50, VC_1 becomes VC_2 and TC_1 becomes TC_2. Assuming no changes to fixed costs and total revenue, this changes the breakeven output to 6,000 units.

> **Key term**
>
> **margin of safety:** the difference between the actual output and the breakeven output.

In our example, if actual output is 12,000 units and the breakeven output is 4,000 units, the margin of safety is 8,000 units (12,000 – 4,000). After variable costs increase, the margin of safety falls to 6,000 units (12,000 – 6,000).

Usefulness of breakeven analysis to start-up businesses

Breakeven analysis is useful to a new business in many ways:

- A new firm can use breakeven analysis to calculate how long it will take to reach the level of output needed to make a profit.

- As a result, the business can predict its likely profit level.
- Breakeven analysis is particularly important to start-up businesses as it is a simple, straightforward way of discovering whether a business plan is likely to succeed financially.
- These data can be used as a key element in persuading bank managers or investors to give financial support to the start-up.
- Usually a start-up will use breakeven analysis to plan its expected results but also a 'best case' scenario and a 'worst case' scenario. This information can indicate the level of risk involved in the start-up.
- Breakeven analysis allows a firm to use 'what if?' analysis to show the different breakeven outputs and the changes in levels of profit that might arise from changes in its price or fixed costs or variable costs.
- The calculations are quick and easy to complete, thus saving businesses time.

Weaknesses of breakeven analysis

Breakeven analysis has the following drawbacks:

- The information may be unreliable.
- The assumption that sales will equal output is a major weakness of breakeven analysis. It is likely that some output will remain unsold.
- In practice, the selling price may change as more is bought and sold.
- Fixed costs may not stay the same as output changes. At particular levels of output, new machines and even new buildings may need to be purchased.
- The analysis assumes that variable costs per unit are always the same, ignoring factors such as buying in bulk.

Analysis

Opportunities for analysis are:

- examining the impact of changes in costs, price and output on contribution and contribution per unit
- understanding how start-up businesses may use contribution to make business decisions
- using 'what if?' analysis to show the impact of different costs and prices on breakeven and profit
- making a decision on a start-up based on these data
- explaining the usefulness and strengths of breakeven analysis
- explaining the limitations and weaknesses of breakeven analysis

Evaluation

Opportunities for evaluation are:

- showing awareness of the strengths and weaknesses of breakeven analysis to a particular business
- making decisions on whether to start a business based on contribution calculations and/or breakeven analysis
- evaluating the best way of reaching breakeven output
- using breakeven analysis to advise on the best way to increase profit

The topics in all sections of Unit 1 have financial repercussions that will affect contribution and breakeven. The notion of contribution per unit is based on similar principles to adding value. Breakeven is used to make decisions on location. This section develops from costs, prices and profit, and most closely links with the remainder of financial planning. It is also vital in assessing the financial success or failure of a business start-up.

Using cash-flow forecasting

Key terms

cash flow: the amounts of money flowing into and out of a business over a period of time.

cash inflows: receipts of cash, typically arising from sales of items, payments by debtors, loans received, rent charged, sale of assets and interest received.

cash outflows: payments of cash, typically arising from the purchase of items, payments to creditors, loans repaid or given, rental payments, purchase of assets and interest payments.

net cash flow: the sum of cash inflows to an organisation minus the sum of cash outflows over a period of time.

cash-flow cycle: the regular pattern of inflows and outflows of cash within a business.

The cash-flow cycle

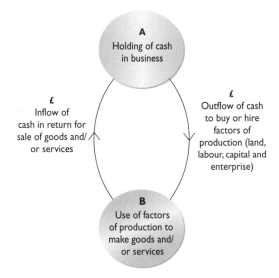

A
Holding of cash in business

£
Inflow of cash in return for sale of goods and/ or services

£
Outflow of cash to buy or hire factors of production (land, labour, capital and enterprise)

B
Use of factors of production to make goods and/ or services

The diagram indicates that there is a delay between outflows of cash and inflows of cash. This means that it is in the nature of business activity that a typical business will suffer cash-flow problems. The extent to which this is a problem will depend on a number of important factors:

- the amount of cash held at the beginning of the cash-flow cycle
- the length of time required to convert inputs into outputs
- the level of credit payments by customers
- the amount of credit offered by suppliers

How to forecast cash flow

Key terms

cash-flow forecasting: the process of estimating the expected cash inflows and cash outflows over a period of time. Cash flow is often seasonal, so it is advisable to forecast for a period of 1 year.

cash-flow statement: a description of how cash flowed into and out of a business during a particular period of time.

A cash-flow forecast attempts to predict the future whereas a cash-flow statement describes what actually happened in the past.

Sources of information

In order to compile a cash-flow forecast, a business uses a number of sources:

- previous cash-flow forecasts
- recent cash-flow statements
- consumer research
- study of similar businesses (e.g. competitors)
- banks
- consultants
- the cash-flow forecast itself — it is important that early drafts of the cash-flow forecast are used to build up the final forecast

Possible causes of inaccuracy

The following problems may cause inaccuracy in a cash-flow forecast:

- changes in the economy
- changes in consumer tastes
- inaccurate market research
- actions by competitors
- uncertainty

Structure of a cash-flow forecast

The details of cash-flow forecasts will vary according to the type of business. However, the key items in constructing a cash-flow forecast are as follows:

- **Cash inflows** (e.g. income from sales).
- **Cash outflows** (e.g. wages and purchases of materials).

- **Net cash flow.** The formula for net cash flow is:
  net cash flow = cash inflows – cash outflows
- **Opening balance and closing balance.** The formula for closing balance is:
  closing cash balance = opening cash balance + net cash flow

A simplified cash-flow forecast is set out in the following table.

	October 2009	November 2009	December 2009
Opening balance	0	4,830	10,120
Total inflows	17,600	18,000	25,000
Materials	5,000	5,200	8,100
Wages	6,200	6,200	6,600
Other costs	1,570	1,310	1,420
Total outflows	12,770	12,710	16,120
Net monthly balance (or flow)	4,830	5,290	8,880
Closing balance	4,830	10,120	19,000

Why businesses forecast cash flow

Key term

liquidity: the ability to convert an asset into cash without loss or delay. The most liquid asset that a business can possess is cash. A cash-flow forecast enables the firm to see possible times in the future when the firm will be short of liquidity. If shortages are anticipated far enough in advance, the firm may be able to take measures that will prevent the shortage from occurring.

The main reasons for forecasting cash flow are:
- to identify potential cash-flow problems in advance
- to guide the firm towards appropriate action
- to make sure that there is sufficient cash available to pay suppliers and creditors and to make other payments
- to provide evidence in support of a request for financial assistance (e.g. asking a bank for an overdraft)
- to avoid the possibility of the company being forced out of business (into liquidation) because of a forthcoming shortage of money
- to identify the possibility of holding too much cash — this probably means that a firm has less machinery and stock than it could possess, which gives the firm less output and stock to sell, so it makes less profit

Analysis

Opportunities for analysis are:
- recognising the significance of the figures in a cash-flow forecast

- analysing the significance of changes in figures in a cash-flow forecast
- understanding the sources of information for cash-flow forecasts
- explaining the reasons for the business forecasting its cash flow
- examining the difficulties in forecasting cash flow for a business start-up

Evaluation

Opportunities for evaluation are:

- evaluating the best sources of information for cash-flow forecasts
- understanding the significance of the data in a cash-flow forecast
- assessing the usefulness of a cash-flow forecast to the business
- judging whether a financial trend (e.g cash flow) is within a firm's control
- weighing up the most likely causes of potential difficulties indicated by a cash-flow forecast

Links

The cash-flow forecast is an essential element of a business plan and the figures in it are derived from estimates relating to all of the other decisions made by the entrepreneur, such as how inputs will be transformed into outputs, how much will be spent on market research, what legal structure the business will select, how finance will be raised and where the business will be located. Cash-flow forecasts are most closely linked to the budgeting process, as this is the other major example of financial planning incorporated into Unit 1.

Setting budgets

Key terms

budget: an agreed plan establishing, in numerical or financial terms, the policy to be pursued and the anticipated outcomes of that policy.

income budget: the agreed, planned income of a business (or division of a business) over a period of time. It may also be described as a revenue budget or sales budget.

expenditure budget: the agreed, planned expenditure of a business (or division of a business) over a period of time.

profit budget: the agreed, planned profit of a business (or division of a business) over a period of time.

Types of budget

Income budgets

The income budget should include income from sales but also other sources of income, such as rent received, if property is owned, or sponsorship, if financial payments are being made by another firm that is using the business's activity for publicity purposes.

Expenditure budgets

Costs that may be found in an expenditure budget include:

- raw materials/components
- labour costs
- marketing expenditure
- administration costs
- rent
- capital costs

For start-ups it is often useful to create a separate expenditure budget, showing the items that must be budgeted for when starting a business. These include premises, furniture, vehicles, insurance and consultancy fees.

Profit budgets

Profit budgets are the result of taking the income budget and subtracting the expenditure budget. They must be scrutinised carefully to ensure that the business is planning activities that are financially viable. Constant review is always required to ensure that problems are not arising.

Budgets are usually stated in terms of financial targets, relating to money allocated to support the organisation of a particular function. However, they also include targets for income, output, sales volume and profit. Budget holders will try to exceed targets for income and profit budgets, whereas for cost budgets (expenditure budgets), of course, the aim is to stay within the planned target.

Planning a budget

Planning a budget involves eight stages:

Stage 1: Set objectives.

Stage 2: Carry out market research into demand and price.

Stage 3: Carry out research into costs.

Stage 4: Complete the sales (income) budget — this will give the business an idea of how much needs to be produced.

Stage 5: Construct the expenditure budget based on this level of production.

Stage 6: Combine stages 4 and 5 to set a profit budget.

Stage 7: Draw up divisional or departmental budgets (usually delegated to managers).

Stage 8: Summarise these budgets in the master budget.

Completing budgets

You should practise completing and amending budgets. For example:

Look at the budget for Trigger Ltd for 2010.

Amend the budget to take into consideration the following changes:

(1) Budgeted income is expected to rise by £43,000.

(2) Wages are expected to increase by 6%.

(3) Raw material costs should increase by 10%.

(4) Other costs will fall by £2,000.

Item	Original budget (£000s)
Budgeted income	578
Wages	150
Raw materials	210
Other costs	103
Budgeted expenditure	463
Budgeted profit	115

Example budget for Trigger Ltd, 2010

(The answer is given on p. 63.)

Methods of setting a budget

There are several methods of setting a budget:

- **Budgeting according to company objectives.** The more ambitious the objectives, the greater the budget that needs to be allocated.
- **Budgeting according to competitors' spending.** In order to stay competitive, a business may have to match the spending of its rivals.
- **Setting the budget as a percentage of sales revenue.** Although this is less scientific, it is commonly used because it is seen to be fair.
- **Zero budgeting/budgeting based on expected outcomes.** In effect, this method allocates a budget on the strength of the case presented by the product manager.
- **Budgeting according to last year's budget allocation.** The logic behind this approach is that, if it was suitable last year, it will be suitable this year.

Reasons for setting budgets

Budgets serve a number of purposes:

- to gain financial support from bank managers and other investors
- to control spending so that a business does not overspend
- to establish priorities by allocating larger budgets to important activities
- to encourage delegation and to motivate staff
- to assign responsibility and so make it much easier to trace mistakes or recognise to whom credit should be given
- to improve efficiency

Problems in setting budgets

Setting budgets involves a number of potential pitfalls:

- Managers may not know enough about the division or department.
- Gathering information can be difficult for a start-up business.
- There may be unforeseen changes.
- The level of inflation (price rises) is not easy to predict.
- Setting a budget can be time consuming.

Item	Amended budget (£000s)
Budgeted income	621
Wages	159
Raw materials	231
Other costs	101
Budgeted expenditure	491
Budgeted profit	130

Amended budget for Trigger Ltd, 2010

Analysis

Opportunities for analysis are:

- demonstrating the process of setting budgets
- explaining the reasons for setting budgets
- analysing the problems involved in setting budgets
- recognising potential reasons why budget estimates may not be reliable
- analysing the significance to the business of a change in a budget

Evaluation

Opportunities for evaluation are:

- evaluating the usefulness of planning budgets
- arguing the relative importance of the different reasons for setting a budget, in a particular situation
- evaluating the main problems in setting a budget
- weighing up the most probable causes of potential difficulties indicated by a budget

Links

Budgeting is another integral element of Unit 1. An understanding of the market enables the income budget to be estimated. The expenditure budget will consist of budgets for inputs, the production process, marketing expenditure, the expenditure involved in choosing a location and the costs of employing people. Consequently, this topic integrates comprehensively with all functions of the business. Finally, the overall assessment of the business start-up may be based on a judgement of whether the profit budget is sufficient.

Assessing business start-ups

Objectives of business start-ups

The objectives of business start-ups vary and depend very much on the individual entrepreneur's motivation. Some examples of objectives are:
- to gain more freedom at work
- to make money
- to grow the business
- to sustain a going concern such as a family business
- to provide employment for the local community

Assessing the business idea and/or plan

The business plan will be useful for reflecting on the strengths and weaknesses of the start-up. Possible issues to consider are:
- what the business's objectives are
- which product or service to provide and whether it can be produced and supplied profitably
- customers' needs and wants, and which market segment to target
- the possibility of competition and an appropriate pricing and selling strategy
- raising finance for day-to-day and longer-term operations
- who will be involved, what they will be doing and what skills, expertise and experience they have
- the risks involved
- is there anything special, new or different about the product that would make it appeal to consumers?

Why start-ups can be risky and why they may fail

New businesses face an enormous number of problems. Approximately one-third of all new firms cease trading within 24 months. The most common problems faced by start-ups are:
- poor cash-flow management
- lack of effective planning
- lack of effective market research
- lack of skills needed to run a business and lack of business training
- lack of finance to fund the business
- the actions of bigger competitors
- failure to capitalise on a good idea
- difficulties in developing a solid customer base

In addition, once the business is up and running, other problems can arise causing business failure. These include:
- unexpected changes in demand for the product or service

- unexpected changes in costs
- delays in and unavailability of supplies

Financial difficulties: raising finance

The main issues are:
- It can be difficult to raise sufficient finance to get started. A new business has no 'track record', so lenders see it as much more of a risk than an established business.
- This 'risk' leads to higher interest rates being charged in order to balance the risk to the lender.
- Banks will want collateral or security: that is, they will want the owners to put up personal guarantees for any loans, offering their own assets, such as their homes or their business premises. In effect, the owner is taking the risk rather than the lender.

These financial issues can:
- slow growth for the business
- threaten the survival of the business
- affect the productivity of the business
- affect the ability of the business to invest (e.g. in new machinery or premises)
- take up management time in seeking sources of finance
- raise costs, perhaps because a lack of finance means that the business is not operating in the most efficient manner

Financial difficulties: cash flow

Even firms that are profitable sometimes find it impossible to continue trading because they are unable to meet their current debts. Often cash is tied up in stock that cannot be used immediately to pay bills.

It is essential, even for a very profitable business, to ensure that it has enough cash available for its working capital needs. A cash-flow forecast is a necessary part of any business plan.

Competition and the difficulties of building a customer base

The success of a business start-up will be determined by its ability to attract and retain customers. To do this, it will have to offer something more than any of its competitors and to gain customer loyalty.

Factors to consider when trying to encourage customer loyalty include:
- Does the start-up plan provide customers with service that is efficient and meets their expectations?
- Is a good after-sales service and system for dealing effectively with customer complaints in place?
- Has market research provided a good understanding of customers' buying habits?
- Has the business start-up ensured that it has adequate resources available (e.g. stock and staff)?
- Is the business aware of any legal requirements for the business?

Analysis

Opportunities for analysis are:

- establishing the main objectives of the business start-up, based on a particular case study
- examining reasons why different objectives may be chosen by an entrepreneur
- explaining the reasons for the success or failure of a particular business start-up
- analysing the strengths or weaknesses of a business idea/plan
- suggesting reasons why a particular start-up might be a risky proposition
- deciding on factors that might lead to a start-up business failing

Evaluation

Opportunities for evaluation are:

- showing awareness of the main objectives of a particular start-up
- evaluating the key factors that have influenced the objectives set by a particular business start-up
- judging the overall success of a start-up by comparing its performance with its objectives
- comparing and contrasting the main risks involved in a particular start-up
- evaluating the strengths and weaknesses of a specific business idea
- drawing a conclusion about the main reasons why a business start-up may fail or may have failed
- recognising the extent to which a business's success or failure has depended on factors within or outside its control

Links

This section draws on every other Unit 1 topic in order to make an overall judgement on whether the basic business idea is sound or risky. It therefore links with every other section, as information about any aspect of the business may be required to make an assessment of the likely success of a business start-up.

Questions
&
Answers

In this section of the guide there are six examination papers. These take the form of a mini-case study followed by two exam-style questions. For each question there are one or two sample answers interspersed by examiner comments.

Questions

You should attempt the case studies on completion of the relevant topics. Case studies 1–5 each cover three topic areas. Case study 6 covers the entire Unit 1 specification.

Case study 1 combines the first three topics of the AQA specification: 'Enterprise', 'Generating and protecting business ideas' and 'Transforming resources into goods and services'. Once you have learned/revised these topics, you will be in a position to test yourself on them.

Case study 2 focuses on the next three topics in the specification: 'Developing business plans', 'Conducting start-up market research' and 'Understanding markets'.

Case study 3 then deals with three of the four remaining topics: 'Choosing the right legal structure for the business', 'Locating the business' and 'Employing people'.

Case study 4 focuses on 'Raising finance', 'Calculating costs, revenues and profits' and 'Using breakeven analysis to make decisions'.

Case study 5 looks at 'Financial planning', i.e. 'Using cash-flow forecasting', 'Setting budgets' and 'Assessing business start-ups'.

Case study 6 is a fully integrated case study, for final revision purposes and includes topics from across the whole specification.

Each case study uses the AQA format. The Unit 1 paper is a 75-minute examination. You are advised to spend 10 minutes reading the mini-case study and questions. This will leave you 65 minutes to produce your written answers. A total of 60 marks are allocated to this paper, so you should plan your timing on the basis of a mark a minute.

Sample answers

Resist the temptation to study the answers before you have attempted the questions. In each case, the first answer (by candidate A) is intended to show the type of response that would earn a grade A on that paper. An A grade does not mean perfection — these answers are intended to show the range of responses that can earn high marks. In business studies, it is the quality of the reasoning that is rewarded.

Case studies 1, 2, 4 and 6 also feature answers from candidate B. Candidate B's answers demonstrate responses that warrant a pass, but not at the A-grade level. Read these answers carefully, as they may help you to avoid potential problems in the examination.

Examiner's comments

The examiner's comments are preceded by the icon *e*. They are interspersed in the answers and indicate where credit is due. In the weaker answers, they also point out areas for improvement, specific problems and common errors.

Krishna's Pottery

This case study focuses on 'Enterprise', 'Generating and protecting business ideas' and 'Transforming resources into goods and services'.

Answer all questions   **Time allowed: 1 hour 15 minutes**

Read the case study below and then answer the questions that follow.

Krishna Patak had one main aim — to earn as much money as possible.

Krishna had other aims too. He also wanted independence and an opportunity to use his creative skills. He believed that this would give him an enjoyable time at work. At the age of 18 he realised he could afford to take a risk, because with his A-level grades he could always go to university if his business venture did not succeed.   5

Krishna started working in his father's art studio, but the job turned out to be just painting copies of well-known masterpieces.

Mr Patak, his father, explained that his business was just part of a national chain of franchises that copied well-known paintings for sale in a high-street retailer. The studio would be given a weekly list of paintings that needed to be reproduced and   10 his father's studio would reproduce and deliver them to the shops. It was a tried-and-tested formula that had earned Mr Patak a good living. There was a low level of risk because the franchisor owned the shops and knew which paintings were likely to sell. However, added value was low on each painting, so the business only succeeded because it produced a lot of paintings each week.   15

During a lunch break one day, Krishna discovered a pottery in an adjoining building. His father had originally supplied pottery products to the franchisor but had closed this part of the business as he had found it difficult to find suitable potters. This was Krishna's main interest in art and he was keen to re-establish the pottery. However, he was not keen on reproducing the same piece of pottery time and time again.   20

Mr Patak encouraged Krishna to set up the pottery again but wanted Krishna to look carefully at the two alternatives — a pottery franchise or an independent pottery. He introduced Krishna to a small business consultant, who explained that there were a number of ways in which the government might support his enterprise, particularly as he was a young entrepreneur in an area of high unemployment.   25

The consultant gave good advice to Krishna on setting up his own business. Krishna got figures from his father to find out how much he could earn if he revived the pottery franchise. Table 1 shows forecast data, comparing the pottery franchise and an independent pottery where Krishna would make his own, individual pieces.

	Pottery franchise	Independent pottery
Average selling price	£10	£75
Average cost of bought-in goods and services	£4	£20
Annual sales (units)	4,500	500

Table 1

Krishna was advised that setting up an independent pottery would involve spending   30
money on marketing and that there was no guarantee of sales. However, the work
would be less pressurised and more interesting. The pottery franchise was much less
risky, but the volume of items produced meant that the transformation process would
use more energy and create more waste products and pollution.

Mr Patak pointed out that the pottery franchise had shops in every major town in   35
Britain and a national reputation that would make it much easier to sell the products.
The franchisor also provided nationwide marketing for its products and shops,
although Krishna would have to pay the delivery costs to the shops.

However, Krishna's father was impressed by Krishna's designs and believed that he
might be able to get a higher price than £75 for some of the pottery pieces Krishna   40
had designed. Krishna's plan was to provide personalised, commemorative pieces of
pottery to celebrate occasions such as weddings and births. He would market them
in the local town through the local radio station, adverts in the local paper and posters
displayed in local stores. On his father's advice, Krishna made sure that his designs
were copyrighted. He had also invented an original process that blended ink on the   45
pottery pieces and with his father's help he took out a patent on this process.

Krishna had a decision to make!

Questions

1 (a) **State three inputs or resources that Krishna might use in the
     transformation process.**   (3 marks)
   (b) **Identify three examples of government support for enterprise or
     entrepreneurs, such as Krishna.**   (3 marks)
   (c) **Calculate the difference between the forecast amount of 'added value'
     on a piece of pottery made by the independent pottery and the 'added
     value' from a piece of pottery made by the pottery franchise.**   (4 marks)
   (d) **If Krishna had decided to set up the pottery franchise, what would
     have been the opportunity cost of this decision?**   (4 marks)
   (e) **Explain two undesirable effects that might result from the transformation
     process involved in converting raw materials into finished pottery.** (6 marks)
2 (a) **Analyse the reasons why Krishna decided to copyright his designs
     and patent his invention.**   (11 marks)

(b) Do you believe that Krishna has the right qualities and characteristics to be a successful entrepreneur? Justify your view. (13 marks)

(c) Discuss whether Krishna should choose to set up a pottery franchise or an independent pottery. (16 marks)

■ ■ ■

Answer to case study 1: candidate A

1 (a) The pottery kiln, Krishna the entrepreneur and Krishna the worker.

☑ Candidate A clearly understands the notion of inputs. However, it is a risky strategy to put Krishna as both an entrepreneur and a worker. This approach should only be used if the candidate cannot genuinely think of a third answer.

(b) ● reducing business taxes
  ● reducing business regulations
  ● introducing legislation to promote competition
  ● guaranteeing bank loans for some entrepreneurs
  ● statistical data provided by DBERR

☑ All of these answers are acceptable. A precise knowledge of detailed support is not required by the examination board. The candidate has wasted a little time by providing five answers when only three were required.

(c) The added value for the independent pottery is £75 – £20 = £55.

The added value for the franchise pottery is £10 – £4 = £6.

The difference between these figures is £55 – £6 = £49.

☑ This answer shows good examination technique because all of the working out is clearly illustrated. Full marks are earned for a correct answer.

(d) The opportunity cost is the next best alternative forgone — what has Krishna given up by setting up the pottery franchise? One thing he has given up is the prospect of going to university, so this is the opportunity cost of his decision.

☑ This is an excellent answer. Candidate A commences with a definition of opportunity cost and then proceeds to apply it in the context of the case study. It is arguable whether going to university was the **next best** alternative forgone, but in the context of this case Krishna was faced with a number of choices and this would be deemed to be an acceptable answer because it clearly shows an understanding of opportunity cost in the context of Krishna's pottery.

(e) The first undesirable effect from the transformation process is the fact that Krishna might get bored. Producing the same item time and time again would not be a very rewarding use of his time.

Second is the amount of waste created by the process — this means a loss of valuable resources and would be considered to be undesirable. Krishna should try to recycle his waste products to make sure that this does not occur.

🖉 The first argument is valid if the franchise was chosen. The second argument includes a recommendation that is not required — a common error in examinations. This is the only answer so far not to produce maximum marks.

2 (a) A patent protects a business from someone copying its invention. It gives the owner a monopoly for 16 to 20 years; this means no competition and so Krishna should make a good profit. It is also possible to make money by selling the patent to another business. As Krishna is operating a very small firm, larger pottery businesses may be interested in buying his patent or licensing it for their own businesses. I would advise Krishna to try to exploit this opportunity.

A patent usually means the product is unique and therefore it is possible that Krishna may be able to sell his pottery at a much higher price. This is also a benefit of getting copyright on the products. If no one can copy your designs, the only place where they can be purchased from is your business. This will enable Krishna to add value and it is almost certain that the very high added value for the independent pottery comes about because of the unique design. Ultimately Krishna should be able to sell more pottery at higher prices and therefore achieve his main aim of making a lot of money.

🖉 This is a very comprehensive answer, showing a clear understanding of patents and following this up with a couple of lines of argument that are very closely related to the situation in the case study. Consequently, it scores well on both application and analysis

(b) I believe that Krishna does have the right characteristics to be a successful entrepreneur. His father is an entrepreneur with a successful business, so it is likely that Krishna has learned from the family's experience. Krishna's father has shown a willingness to help and appears to have good contacts. In the case study, Krishna has benefited from using expert advice.

Most importantly, in my opinion, Krishna has clear aims. At the beginning of the case study he is focused on making a lot of money and this will provide him with an incentive to work hard — an important quality in any entrepreneur.

Krishna is also creative and an original thinker, as shown by his ability to get a patent and create original designs. However, Krishna does not appear to have any financial backing. He is very heavily dependent on his father's financial support and, as a school leaver, he lacks experience at the age of 18. Although he may be a good potter, this does not guarantee success because an entrepreneur must have business skills in other areas too, such as marketing and accounting, particularly if he is operating as a sole trader.

In evaluation, I feel that Krishna does have the ability to succeed, as it is the quality of the pottery that will ultimately help him to build a customer base. However, he may need to employ specialist help in some of the more general business skills such as accountancy.

This is an excellent answer, drawing well upon the case study and providing good, logical reasons to support the arguments presented. The final paragraph shows good examination technique. In longer questions, candidates sometimes forget to draw up a balanced argument. Candidate A starts the last paragraph with the words 'In evaluation'. This approach will tend to lead to an evaluative conclusion.

(c) There are some compelling arguments for Krishna to take the independent pottery option. Independence is one of Krishna's aims and this will provide him with that target, as well as giving him scope for creativity and an interesting job — both of which were also important to him.

Krishna's main aim was to make money and the very high added value for the independent pottery should mean that there is greater scope to achieve this target. Of course, this comes with a great deal of risk, as there is at present no certain market for this type of pottery.

Another major factor to consider is that Krishna has achieved a patent and has acquired copyright. If he chose the franchise, he would be unable to benefit from these major advantages.

It is not clear what skills Krishna possesses outside his pottery skills and this could be a reason why he should go for the franchise option, which appears to be safe and secure. He will make £6 per product and there is the potential to make a lot of money without much risk. However, I'm not sure that Krishna would be able to sustain this type of business, particularly knowing that he could have set up independently.

My advice to him is to carry out some market research and get help in carrying out the office functions (perhaps from his father's business). He can go ahead with the independent pottery which will meet all of his main aims and use his skills to the full.

An excellent, evaluative answer throughout, drawing upon the main arguments and explaining them using good business logic and application to the case study. The final conclusion is a natural development from the arguments presented.

Candidate A has produced an outstanding script, almost achieving maximum marks. This would be a clear A grade.

■ ■ ■

Answer to case study 1: candidate B

1 (a) Land, labour, enterprise and capital.

🖉 Although this is a generic list of the factors of production, it does technically answer the question. It is usually advisable to be as precise as possible, so this answer would have been better if specific examples of each of these factors of production had been provided.

(b) —

🖉 Candidate B has not answered this question. It is worth going back to answer a question that you have left blank, if time permits at the end of the exam. A guess may yield a mark or two.

(c) £49

🖉 This answer is correct and receives full marks, but it does not show good examination technique. If candidate B had made a minor error in working out the answer, it would have been impossible for the examiner to have detected this mistake. Consequently, the examiner would have been forced to give this answer zero marks as it would have demonstrated no understanding. The examiner can only mark what they see, so calculation should always be shown.

(d) The independent pottery.

🖉 Again this is an example of poor examination technique. It is almost certain that candidate B understands the notion of opportunity cost because the independent pottery is the expected right answer. However, the examination board is not going to give 4 marks for three words and the expectation of the examination board is that there will be an explanation of what is meant by opportunity cost.

(e) According to the case study, 'The pottery franchise was much less risky but the volume of items produced meant that the transformation process would use more energy and create more waste products and pollution.'

🖉 Be careful when using the case study. It is a very useful source of information to answer questions, but it is unlikely that merely copying an extract from the case study is answering the question set. Candidate B is making a common error. Having identified the right part of the case study on which to base the answer, candidate B has not then addressed the question, which was to show why these factors were undesirable effects. However, because the correct ideas have been identified, a couple of knowledge marks would have been earned for recognising that using energy and creating waste products and pollution are the undesirable effects.

2 (a) Copyright protects the business from someone using their designs. This is obviously a benefit for any business and would have helped Krishna.

Patents are given for inventions and prevent other businesses from copying an invention. This would have helped Krishna.

e Candidate B understands both copyright and patents, and earns full marks for content/knowledge. However, candidate B is merely stating that this helps the business and is not demonstrating how in any way. Therefore no further marks would be awarded.

(b) Krishna is unlikely to be successful as an entrepreneur. He has only just left school and has no idea about the business world. So far, he has been lucky that he has had support from his father. Krishna will have very little understanding of the business world and being an entrepreneur requires many skills. Krishna appears to be very limited as the only skill he appears to have relates to the pottery. Problems such as cash-flow difficulties often cause the downfall of new businesses and Krishna will have no experience of dealing with these problems when they inevitably arise.

e There are some good arguments in this answer, but candidate B has let themselves down by trying to prove their point too forcefully. All of the arguments presented have some validity, but candidate B seems to have focused on Krishna's inexperience and chosen to ignore any arguments that might counterbalance this weakness. In evaluative questions, it is normally better to weigh up strengths and weaknesses and draw an objective conclusion, based on the balance of arguments in the answer.

(c) Arguments for the pottery franchise:
- there is less risk in a franchise
- the franchisor carries out the marketing
- there is a guaranteed market through the franchisor's shops

Arguments for the independent pottery:
- this option matches Krishna's aim for independence
- it uses the copyrights and patents systems

There are three arguments for the pottery franchise and two for the independent business, so I would advise Krishna to go with the franchise.

e It is not a sensible idea to use bullet points in your answers, as they encourage brevity. Candidate B has identified a range of appropriate arguments for both options but has failed to develop these points. The use of a scoring system for evaluation is not appropriate because it ignores the relative strengths of each argument.

Overall this script would have gained an E grade. In places, candidate B shows good understanding, but poor examination technique means that a number of opportunities to cash in on this understanding have been missed. With better technique, candidate B could have improved this grade.

The Crechton Crèche

This case study focuses on 'Developing business plans', 'Conducting start-up market research' and 'Understanding markets'.

Answer all questions   **Time allowed: 1 hour 15 minutes**

Read the case study below and then answer the questions that follow.

Sofia was ecstatic! The bank manager had studied her business plan and agreed to give her a loan and an overdraft. He had complimented her on the quality of her business plan. Her plan to open in January 2009 was on course.

Her friend Becky was also planning to open a crèche and asked to see a summary of Sofia's plan (see Table 1).   5

Business plan for the Crechton Crèche	
Location	High Street, Crechton
Objectives of business	To provide a safe environment for young children in central Crechton To achieve a profit target of £6,000 per annum by 2011
Personal details: owner and manager	Sofia Mancini. Age 21 Qualifications: 9 GCSEs grade A*–C; CACHE Diploma 3 years' FT experience as a nursery nurse
Assets owned	Wide range of crèche equipment, furniture, toys and games
Other assets	5-year lease of community hall with free car parking
Capacity	32 children in 2009 (24 needed to make a profit) Capacity to be expanded to 50 children by 2012
Staffing	This would vary according to the number of children but would be in accordance with government requirements for ratios of staff to children.
Summary of profit forecasts	2009: loss of £5,000 2010: profit of £1,000 2011: profit of £8,000 2012: profit of £13,000 with further growth expected (Profit calculated after allowing for Sofia's wages and loan repayment)
Financial sources	75% of capital: owner and loans from family 25% of capital: bank loan

Table 1 Sofia's business plan

Originally the bank manager had turned down Sofia's request because of the lack of a marketing plan. Sofia had worked hard to try to put this right.

Her first action was to look at some secondary market research details from the local council. These figures showed the age distribution of the population of Crechton and

the number of children in crèches over the last 10 years. This indicated to Sofia that   10
in 2009 there was a potential target market of 400 children in crèches in Crechton.
By 2012 the number of children in crèches was expected to reach 460.

Sofia's primary market research was more varied. Firstly, she used her experience
from the crèche at which she had been working for the last 3 years, in order to decide
on how to equip and run the crèche. Secondly, she asked parents and children what   15
they liked most about the crèche, and to give her suggestions on how it could be
improved. This gave Sofia some useful insights into how she could provide a much
better crèche than the one at which she had been working.

Sofia followed this up with a focus group, where she invited some young mothers to
a brainstorming session. They exchanged ideas on what they wanted most from a   20
crèche. Finally, Sofia stood in the High Street one weekend, close to where she
intended to set up the business, and asked passers-by. She felt that this would be very
useful because they would be the people who lived locally. However, in the end this
proved to be less useful because her customers turned out to be people who worked
in the High Street on weekdays whereas her questions had been asked to Saturday   25
shoppers. This created some difficulties at first, because Sofia's opening hours did not
match the working hours of her customers, who wanted the crèche to stay open for
much longer than she had planned.

This led Sofia to think carefully about the usefulness of market segmentation.
Originally she had intended to serve the needs of people who lived in the centre of   30
the town, believing that they would be prepared to pay higher prices for crèche
facilities. However, her new market segment of High Street workers provided even
more opportunities, as they were generally families where both the husband and wife
worked. They worked mostly in financial services occupations, so they were prepared
to pay high prices for the quality service that Sofia offered. It was also easy to target   35
this market because she could promote her services by direct communication with a
number of key employers. These companies were only too grateful to pass on
information that would make it easier for their employees to find crèche facilities.

Sofia was confident that her business would expand because she was offering a price
that undercut most of her competitors. The population of Crechton was growing.   40
Crechton was a successful centre for financial services and was attracting a number
of growing businesses that brought in wealthy families with young children. Sofia
also believed that she could capture the tourist market. Crechton was a historic town
with lots of visitors. Her long-term plan was to open on Saturdays and Sundays for
weekend visitors and to target the tourist market by offering crèche facilities for   45
holidaymakers during the summer.

Questions

1 (a) **Identify two sources of information for a business plan.**   (2 marks)
   (b) **State one example of qualitative market research used by Sofia.**   (1 mark)
   (c) **What is meant by the term 'secondary market research' (line 8)?**   (3 marks)

(d) **Calculate the percentage rate of market growth expected between 2009 and 2012.** (3 marks)

(e) **Assuming that Sofia's crèche is working at full capacity, calculate Sofia's market share of the crèche market in Crechton in 2009.** (3 marks)

(f) **Explain three factors that might lead to an increase in demand for Sofia's crèche.** (8 marks)

2 (a) **Analyse the benefits to Sofia of using market segmentation in the planning of the crèche.** (10 marks)

(b) **Evaluate the strengths and weaknesses of Sofia's sampling methods.** (14 marks)

(c) **To what extent would Sofia's business plan have been vital in determining the level of success of her crèche?** (16 marks)

■ ■ ■

Answer to case study 2: candidate A

1 **(a)** Market research; the owner's business experience.

e Two correct answers related to the information in the case study.

(b) The focus group.

e Correct.

(c) Secondary market research is data that has already been collected for a different purpose but which is adapted for use by a business.

e A clear and concise definition that earns full marks.

(d) Market growth (%) is $\dfrac{460 - 400}{400} \times 100 = \dfrac{60}{400} \times 100 = 15\%$

e Full marks for a correct answer with the added benefit of a clear presentation of the calculations.

(e) market share = $\dfrac{24}{400} \times 100 = 6\%$

e Candidate A has taken the breakeven number (24) instead of the full-capacity figure (32). However, because the working out is clear and candidate A has made only a minor error, 2 of the 3 marks can be awarded, because candidate A clearly understands market share. The answer should have been 8%.

(f) Firstly, the price set. Sofia's charges were lower than those of her competitors. This might not be a major factor in the case of crèches, but families may be very price conscious because crèche costs can take up a large chunk of a weekly income. For this reason Sofia might gain a lot of extra customers by being slightly cheaper than her rivals.

A second factor influencing the demand is the population of Crechton. With lots of rich young families, consumer incomes would be high and this would encourage people to spend more on local services such as crèches. Putting a child in the crèche would also enable both parents to work and could therefore increase their incomes considerably.

Thirdly, the location of Sofia's business in the High Street was ideal to people working in the local shops and the financial services businesses. Although initially Sofia may have lost these customers by offering insufficient hours, she rectified this problem by extending the hours to suit the needs of her customers. The fact that the crèche had free parking would have also helped people who were trying to use the crèche for their children.

This is an excellent answer with three factors analysed effectively and applied in a relevant way to Sofia's crèche.

2 **(a)** Market segmentation has been very useful to Sofia. It has helped her to target her marketing at the customers who will use her services; in this case it is the workers in the High Street who are looking for places for their children while they are at work. Through market segmentation, Sofia has been able to discover the exact needs of this group of people and has adjusted the opening hours to suit them. Sofia originally targeted mothers of the crèche where she had worked and found out some very useful information on the facilities that she should put in her new crèche.

Her target market segment worked mostly in financial services occupations, so they were prepared to pay high prices for a crèche. This was helpful to Sofia as it would have allowed her to put up prices without losing customers. By having a clear focus on the market segment, she was also able to market efficiently. In her case she gave information to companies who passed it on to their employees.

Overall, market segmentation allowed Sofia to attract customers, increase her prices and save expenses on marketing.

An excellent set of arguments that focus on the key issues. This answer would earn high marks.

(b) Sofia's market research was very suitable. Her secondary market research gave her a very accurate picture of both the present situation in Crechton and the future growth possibilities. This led to Sofia being able to present a confident case to the bank manager in order to get the financial support that she needed to set up the business.

She then undertook some qualitative market research that gave her an insight into the ways in which she should operate the crèche. However, because the customer base changed it could be argued that this market research was irrelevant and may not have led to her business succeeding.

Overall I think that her secondary market research was good but the primary market research was weak.

⮌ This is unfortunate as candidate A has answered the wrong question. This answer is about market research, but the question required a focus on the sampling methods used. Therefore, although the answer seems to flow naturally it is not addressing the question set. It is vital that you read the question carefully before committing to an answer, particularly on a question such as 2(b), which carries a maximum of 14 marks.

(c) Sofia's business plan was very helpful. By having clear objectives it will allow her to compare the progress of the business against targets, so that she can see if the business is failing or succeeding. If she falls short of these objectives — for example, if the business does not reach a profit by the end of the second year — then Sofia can take actions to try to rectify this problem.

By looking at the details not shown in the business summary plan, she may be able to detect where the problems are arising and put them right.

The most obvious use of the plan was in persuading the bank manager to decide on whether Sofia's business should be backed. The vital significance of the plan can be shown by the fact that the bank manager originally refused to lend money because the business plan was not adequate, but when Sofia presented a much better plan a loan was agreed. Without this loan it is unlikely that Sofia could have set up the business and so it would not have succeeded.

In order to complete a business plan, Sofia had to show that she had done some careful market research and had a good marketing plan. It was this activity that allowed her to finally discover the best customer base and one that would almost certainly lead to success for her crèche.

In conclusion, it is clear that elements of the business plan will be vital for the future success of the business. However, it should be noted that the business has not yet started and the key to success will be how well Sofia implements her business plan. Although the plan is a critical element, there are many other factors that influence its final success.

⮌ A comprehensive answer, rooted in the context of the case study and showing judgement throughout.

Candidate A has fallen down badly in question 2(b), but every other response has been excellent. An A grade does not require perfection and this script would achieve a grade A overall.

■ ■ ■

Answer to case study 2: candidate B

1 (a) Accountants; small business advisors

⮌ Neither of these sources is mentioned in the case study, but the wording of the question is such that a link to the case is not required. Some early questions in

Unit 1 require general understanding of the specification and may not need direct application. Consequently, candidate B would earn both marks.

(b) Census of Population data.

🗩 This answer is incorrect in two respects: the Census of Population provides quantitative data and there is no mention of it in the case study. This question required an example from the case study.

(c) Secondary market research is data that has been collected in order to help a business understand its market. A disadvantage of secondary market research is that it may be dated.

🗩 The first line of this definition could apply to both secondary and primary market research. In fact it is a definition of market research. Consequently, this cannot be credited. However, the second sentence does give some indication that it was secondary market research that was being considered and the mark scheme would award 1 mark for 'some' understanding. It is quite common for a vague answer to receive some credit through an additional sentence that makes the candidate's thinking slightly clearer.

(d) Market growth (%) is $\dfrac{460 - 400}{460} \times 100 = \dfrac{60}{460} \times 100 = 13.0\%$

🗩 This answer is incorrect. Candidate B has made a common mistake, dividing the change of 60 by the final market size (460). Percentage changes should be based on the original size (400 in this case). This is only one error and because candidate B has shown their working, it is possible to give credit for the elements of the answer that are correct.

(e) market share (%) = $\dfrac{\text{company's sales}}{\text{total sales in the market}} \times 100$

🗩 There has been no attempt to make a calculation, but 1 mark would be awarded for showing the correct formula. It is possible that candidate B was unable to find the appropriate figures under examination pressure.

(f) Three factors that might influence demand are:
- price
- competitors' actions, and
- the business's marketing

Usually the lower the price, the greater the amount demanded, as a low price makes a product much more attractive to customers. Competitors' actions will normally lead to a reduction in demand, as they will be trying to stop their rivals gaining market share . Marketing is another factor that can increase the demand for a product. An effective advertising campaign on television or in the newspapers will bring in more customers.

📝 Three relevant points have been identified, but they have been explained in a rather general, theoretical way. Furthermore, the second factor has been described as a factor that reduces demand and is therefore not answering the question set. This question requires application to Sofia's crèche and the omission of such references means that it would receive limited credit.

2 **(a)** The usefulness of market segmentation. Originally she had intended to serve the needs of people who lived in the centre of the town, believing that they would be prepared to pay higher prices for crèche facilities. However, her new market segment of High Street workers provided even more opportunities, as they were generally families where both the husband and wife worked. They worked mostly in financial services occupations, so they were prepared to pay high prices for the quality service that Sofia offered. It was also easy to target this market because she could promote her services by direct communication with a number of key employers. These companies were only too grateful to pass on information that would make it easier for their employees to find crèche facilities.

📝 Candidate B has identified the correct part of the case study from which to develop their answer, but rather than genuinely responding to the question they have just copied out the extract from the case study. This is not a valid approach. Although it may be tempting to quote from the case study, any wording must be phrased so that it is responding to the question set. This answer does not meet this requirement.

(b) Sofia used are a very small sample for her focus group. This may seem to be inappropriate, as the larger sample, the more accurate the results. However, because this was a focus group, detailed opinions were needed on what people expected from a crèche and why they liked or disliked a certain crèche. Consequently, I feel that this small group was appropriate, as it would have encouraged people to express more honest and open opinions.

Sofia's sampling for her other market research was poor. She stood in the High Street, which was the right place to get opinions, but at the wrong time. At the weekend she would have picked up shoppers rather than the local residents that she was originally targeting. She then found that it was the local workers who were attracted to her crèche, but her market research sample was still irrelevant to this market segment, and there is no evidence in the case to suggest that Sophia did anything to overcome this weakness.

Overall I think that Sofia's sampling was quite poor because she did not get opinions from the people who would be using her crèche. It could be argued that the focus group would have helped her decide on the right facilities in her crèche, as the business looked likely to succeed. However, she was appealing to richer people and they may have given different responses to the ones she got from her focus group.

e This is an excellent answer to a challenging question. Because there is rather limited information on sampling in the case study, the examiner would make allowances. Candidate B has surpassed expectations by highlighting the two key issues: the focus group and the inappropriate sampling in the High Street.

(c) Business plans are helpful to entrepreneurs as they set clear objectives, letting the entrepreneur measure whether they have been successful or not. Furthermore, the plan would steer the entrepreneur towards strategies or actions needed to meet these objectives.

Sometimes business plans can help to persuade lenders to invest capital in the business by demonstrating why it is likely to succeed. Bank managers will want to see a business plan before giving bank loans or overdrafts. This was the case in Sofia's business.

Business plans can also encourage entrepreneurs to plan ahead in a realistic way. This should help them to succeed.

In evaluation, Sofia's business plan helped her to succeed.

e Some standard arguments are presented here, but only in one instance — when talking about the bank manager – does candidate B draw upon the case study. Consequently, some marks would be given for analysis, but only minimal credit for application. The final sentence is not evaluation because the judgment is not supported by evidence.

Candidate B has provided a mixture of good and weak answers. There are more of the latter than the former, but the excellence of the answer to question 2(b) and the fact that answer 2(c) picks up useful marks puts this script into the high grade D/borderline grade C category.

Case study 3

Fund raising

This case study focuses on 'Choosing the right legal structure for the business', 'Locating the business' and 'Employing people'.

Answer all questions   **Time allowed: 1 hour 15 minutes**

Read the case study below and then answer the questions that follow.

Archie and Kim lived in a big house and enjoyed expensive holidays, but they needed something else. As recently retired lawyers, they felt that it was time to put their knowledge into helping raise money for other people.

They had made a lot of good business contacts but were inexperienced in organising large events, so they decided to seek help from a business adviser who specialised   5
in this sector. Her advice was excellent, especially in terms of employing people. Archie and Kim had intended to employ full-time permanent employees to run the events, but the consultant advised temporary, part-time workers instead. Within 4 weeks Archie and Kim had put on their first charity event to raise money for good causes.   10

They decided that a not-for-profit business would be sensible, as they felt that this would give the business more credibility. There had been recent negative publicity in the national newspapers and on television concerning some fundraising organisations that were making high profits for their owners. Archie and Kim did not really need the money, as they were already wealthy. They also believed that people were more   15
inclined to donate to charities that were not trying to make money from their donors.

At first they operated as a partnership, until a large open-air event made a big loss as a result of unexpectedly bad weather. Archie and Kim had to use their own funds to pay off this loss and soon after they decided to convert to a private limited company. A couple of friends had been involved in similar work as sole traders and were eager   20
to join them. As a limited company, the business was also able to attract a few other investors and this enabled it to put on much bigger events that earned more money for the charities. However, Kim in particular believed that the status of private limited company would make it harder to convince people that they were not aiming to make a profit, especially as new shareholders might outvote her and Archie and change the   25
policy.

Most of the events took place in hotels, which charged high prices to Archie and Kim's business. As a result, a shareholders' meeting was held and it was decided that the business should buy its own hotel. A couple of suitable properties were on the market and Archie and Kim summarised their relative merits (see Table 1).   30

	Grange Hotel (4-star)	White Hart Hotel (4-star)
Location	Country estate	City centre
Transport links	Close to motorway, but poor access to other transport	Close to railway station, taxi rank and bus station
Appearance	High quality, but old-fashioned and run-down	Light and modern; reasonable quality
Fund-raising facilities	Acceptable ballroom; excellent outdoor facilities	Outstanding ballroom; no outdoor facilities
Restaurant	High quality; limited variety of dishes on menu	Acceptable quality; wide-ranging menu
Costs	Cheap to buy, but high running costs	Expensive to buy, but low running costs

Table 1 Comparison of the Grange and White Hart Hotels

Kim looked at the data and said, 'The infrastructure is very important. People like to visit the shops before an event and most of our events have taken place in the city centre because of the transport situation — but can we afford the White Hart? Besides, our customers generally want high-quality food as a priority.'

'Our two most profitable events have been outdoors,' added Archie, 'but our big loss-making event was also outside.'   35

'The problem is that "qualitative" factors are so important to our customers. Some are fussy about the appearance of the hotel and the quality of the food, but others are more interested in whether it is modern or old-fashioned. Ironically, the only factor that seems to be unimportant is the price we charge. They are so keen to donate that   40 they are insulted if we cut the price of an event.'

Questions

1 (a) **What is meant by the term 'sole trader' (line 20)?**   (2 marks)
   (b) **What is meant by the term 'infrastructure' (line 31)?**   (3 marks)
   (c) **Outline the meaning of the term 'qualitative factors' in terms of factors that might influence location decisions, and state one example of a qualitative factor from the case study.**   (4 marks)
   (d) **Explain one reason why Archie and Kim used a consultant to help the business.**   (5 marks)
   (e) **Explain two reasons why Archie and Kim decided to set up a 'not-for-profit' business rather than a business seeking to make profit.**   (6 marks)

2 (a) **Analyse the reasons why the consultant advised Archie and Kim to employ temporary, part-time workers rather than full-time, permanent employees.**   (10 marks)
   (b) **Discuss the reasons behind Archie and Kim's decision to change from a partnership to a private limited company.**   (14 marks)

(c) **Should the business buy the Grange Hotel or the White Hart Hotel?**
   Justify your decision.   (16 marks)

▓ ▓ ▓

Answer to case study 3: candidate A

1 **(a)** A sole trader is a business that is owned by one person.

   ✍ A correct answer that would earn full marks.

(b) This is the network of utilities, e.g. transport links, sewerage, telecommunications systems, health services and educational facilities, in an area.

   ✍ Another correct answer that would earn full marks. It is important that you can
   accurately define business concepts in Unit 1.

(c) Qualitative factors are personal preferences that might affect the location of
   the business, rather than factors based on business principles, such as costs.
   Local sports facilities are an example.

   ✍ The definition would earn full marks, but the question also asked for an example
   from the case study. The example given is not included in the case and cannot
   therefore be credited.

(d) They decided to seek help from a business adviser because they lacked
   experience in fund raising. The consultant was able to give advice that helped
   them to improve their thinking, especially when it came to employing staff.

   ✍ A concise, accurate answer that would score well.

(e) The main reason Archie and Kim set up a not-for-profit business was that they
   didn't need the money. They had already reached the living standard that they
   wanted to achieve and felt that they could give back to society in this way.

   A second reason is that it would give the business more credibility if it was
   seen that the owners were not taking money out. This would encourage donors
   to give generously. It is indicated in the case that donors gave generously,
   possibly as a result of Archie and Kim's own generosity.

   ✍ This response draws upon the text effectively. Candidate A's approach
   demonstrates that they are thinking about the wording of the question and
   showing why Archie and Kim made this decision.

2 **(a)** Temporary workers provide greater flexibility for a business, as they can be
   used as and when they are required. Part-time workers also provide flexibility,
   as they can be called in to work a few hours extra if the business requires it
   and it suits the needs of the worker. This is an unusual business in that it does
   not operate during regular business hours. By putting on occasional fundraising
   events it does not really require a core of full-time staff. In fact it needs the

opposite. Staff are only required when an event is being run. It is probable that these events take place outside working hours so that working people can attend and donate money. This is exactly the time when a part-time worker such as a student may be prepared to work. It may also suit temporary workers, possibly attracted by high hourly rates for unpredictable work.

🖉 This is a difficult question because there is not a lot of supporting evidence in the case study. However, candidate A has used their theoretical knowledge and applied it to the circumstances of the business in order to earn application marks. Overall this is a very good response.

(b) The benefit of converting to a private limited company is limited liability. The couple have already had to subsidise one event which made a loss. Partnerships have unlimited liability and a major disaster could mean that they have to sell valuable assets such as their own personal property. The nature of the business would suggest that they have to put a lot of money into an event before receiving any money back, so big losses could happen if they lose customers. Therefore limited liability is essential.

Buying a hotel is a very expensive undertaking. It is unlikely that Archie and Kim have enough money to be able to afford one. By becoming a private limited company they have brought in new shareholders who may provide this money. Bank managers are more willing to lend money to larger businesses, so they may find it easier to get loans because they are able to provide more security.

A disadvantage is the credibility of the business and this was certainly a factor that Kim was concerned about.

Limited company status may also bring in more people to help operate the business and this could relieve the workload on them.

On balance I think it was the right decision to convert to private limited company status, as it prevents the other owners from losing all their personal possessions. Also the extra money will make this less likely to happen.

🖉 This is a thorough presentation of the advantages of changing from a partnership to a private limited company. There are only limited arguments against and they have not been fully developed in this answer. Evaluation is demonstrated in the final paragraph and also in earlier arguments — most noticeably at the end of the opening paragraph. The answer would have benefited from a more detailed evaluation of the problems.

(c) I would advise them to buy the White Hart.

Although it is much more expensive than the Grange, it meets their requirements more. The majority of their events take place in the city centre because the customers do not want to drive a long distance. The White Hart has much better transport facilities.

It is best not to run a fundraising event in a dark old-fashioned place, such as the Grange. Light and modern facilities are ideally suited to putting the customers in a good mood, ready to hand over lots of cash. Archie and Kim are attracting lots of different customers, so they will want a wide and varied menu that will suit everyone's needs. The quality of the food is something that they can tackle by employing new or retraining old staff, whereas the age of the buildings cannot be changed. If the occasional outdoor event is required, they can still hire a suitable hotel. With the English weather it is much more important to be able to offer indoor events. As long as they can afford to buy the hotel, its running costs will be much lower than the Grange. All of this points to the White Hart being the ideal location.

Despite a slight tendency towards trying to prove their case and ignoring some of the attributes of the Grange, this is still a very good answer that presents a range of reasons supporting the choice of the White Hart.

Candidate A has produced a series of excellent answers. This examination paper would have been awarded a fully merited high grade A.

Shopping for shops

This case study focuses on 'Raising finance', 'Calculating costs, revenues and profits' and 'Using breakeven analysis to make decisions'.

Answer all questions   **Time allowed: 1 hour 15 minutes**

Read the case study below and then answer the questions that follow.

Fàtima was excited about her plan to open a new shop. The final task was to check out the financial forecasts in order to confirm the best option.

Both shops would cost Fàtima £300,000. Fàtima had a number of sources of finance to choose from:

- **Personal savings.** Fàtima and her husband had saved £100,000, which she would   5
  be able to put into the business.
- **Other personal sources.** Her cousin was prepared to lend her £100,000 for 10
  years. He wanted no interest payments for the first 5 years, to help the business
  establish itself, but half the profits made after the fifth year.
- **Bank loan.** The bank manager had agreed to a loan of £100,000 at a fixed rate   10
  of interest of 6% per annum for 5 years. The bank manager was also prepared to
  offer Fàtima an overdraft.
- **Ordinary shares.** Fàtima had decided to set up as a private limited company.
  Two friends were each interested in investing £100,000. Both of them wanted 22%
  of the shares in return.   15
- **Venture capital.** A venture capitalist had agreed to put in £100,000 and offer
  weekly advice to Fàtima in return for a 40% shareholding.

Option 1 was a computer supplies business. Fàtima had good connections and was
able to buy computer supplies at a very low cost. Her supplier had bought cheap
materials from a company that had failed and had enough stock to supply her for 3   20
years. After that the cost of her supplies would increase significantly.

The shop was located in the town centre. Unfortunately, most potential customers
tended to go to the out-of-town shopping centre, as that was where PC World and
Comet were based. Fàtima only expected to pick up passing trade, rather than people
who were deliberately going shopping in order to buy computer supplies. This did   25
have the advantage of allowing her to set quite a high price for her computer supplies,
as these customers were less likely to know the prices being charged by competitors.
Fàtima felt guilty about this but recognised that it was good business.

Fàtima was not really interested in computers but had a number of friends who were
experts and could advise her if she got into difficulties.   30

Option 2 was a toy shop. Fàtima was fascinated by all the new toys available for
young children, and her enjoyment of the day that she spent with the business owner
was surpassed only by that of her children. They had enjoyed a delightful day

occupying themselves in the play area in the shop. Fàtima felt that she might save
some childminding expenses. Her children went to a nearby school and they seemed   35
eager to stay with her in the shop after school until the shop closed at 5.30 p.m. Toy
sales had declined at the expense of computer games in recent years and this had led
to the closure of the main competitor in town. Her shop would be the only specialist
toy shop in the centre of town, although she would be competing with shops such as
Woolworths and WH Smith.   40

Fàtima looked at the forecast finances for the first year of trading of the two shops.

Figure 1 is a breakeven chart for option 1, the computer supplies business.

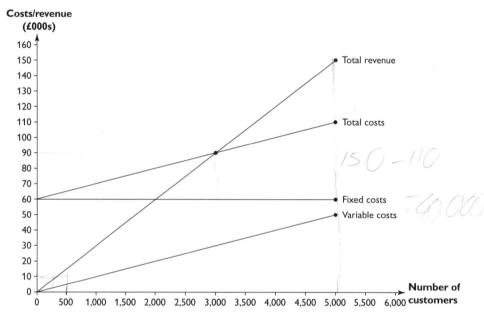

Figure 1 Breakeven chart for the computer supplies business

Table 1 shows the forecast costs, revenue and number of customers for option 2, the
toy shop.

Item	Revenue/costs
Average selling price	£20
Average variable costs	£8
Annual fixed costs	£48,000
Other data	
Forecast number of customers per year: 6,500	

Table 1 Forecast costs, revenue and customers for the toy shop

Questions

1 (a) **What is meant by the term 'overdraft' (line 12)?**   (2 marks)
For each part of 1(b), you should refer to Figure 1, the breakeven chart for option 1, the computer supplies business.
   (b) (i)   **How much are the fixed costs for option 1, the computer supplies business?**   (2 marks)
       (ii) **How much is the level of profit if the business has 5,000 customers?**   (3 marks)
       (iii) **What is the level of the margin of safety if the business has 5,000 customers?**   (3 marks)
       (iv) **How much is the 'total contribution' from 5,000 customers?**   (5 marks)
   (c) **Refer to Table 1. Calculate the breakeven number of customers for option 2, the toy shop.**   (5 marks)
2 (a) **Analyse two ways in which Fàtima might reduce the breakeven output for the toy shop.**   (8 marks)
   (b) **Discuss the sources of finance that Fàtima should choose, in order to raise the £300,000 needed to set up her business.**   (15 marks)
   (c) **Using the information provided in Figure 1 and Table 1 and any other information that you wish to consider, advise Fàtima on which of the two shops she should choose. Justify your view.**   (17 marks)

■ ■ ■

Answer to case study 4: candidate A

1 (a) An overdraft is where a person can 'go into the red'. They can spend more money than they have in their current bank account, up to an agreed limit.

   [2] A very clear definition that would earn full marks.

   (b) (i)   £60,000
       (ii)   £40,000
       (iii) 2,000 customers
       (iv)   £60,000

   [2] This is poor examination technique because no working is shown. Fortunately for candidate A, the first three answers are all correct and so full marks would be earned. However, the final answer is incorrect and because there is no working out the examiner would award no marks. If candidate A had shown some working out, credit could have been given for any calculations that were correct.

   (c) breakeven output = $\dfrac{\text{fixed costs}}{\text{contribution per customer}}$

$$= \frac{£48,000}{£20 - £8} = \frac{£48,000}{£12} = 4,000 \text{ customers}$$

Full marks for an excellent answer.

2 **(a)** Fàtima could reduce the breakeven number of customers by reducing her fixed costs. She may be able to negotiate a lower rent, although this might be quite difficult as the store is in the town centre. If interest rates fall, she may reduce her fixed costs and enable her to reach breakeven with fewer customers. Low-cost shelving may still be able to carry out the function that she needs, but with reduced fixed costs. If she can lower her fixed costs to £36,000 then she will only need 3,000 customers to break even.

Fàtima might increase her prices — £20 does not seem to be excessively high. As she is the only specialist toy shop, she may be able to use this as a unique selling point. By offering good customer service she may be able to increase the contribution per customer.

This is a well-argued response, particularly the first part on fixed costs, which applies the figures in the case study well to answer the question.

(b) I think Fàtima should keep control of her business. Therefore it is essential that she uses personal finance — the £100,000 that she and her husband had saved. She will not need to pay interest on this money, although there is the opportunity cost of how much interest this was earning in the bank or wherever it was being saved. This source of finance is important to Fàtima because it will help her overcome the difficult first year.

I think that Fàtima should also use the £100,000 that her cousin is prepared to lend her. He wanted no interest for the first 5 years, and this will help the business to establish itself. I think she may want to try to negotiate the element about half the profits made after the fifth year — this is a serious drawback of this particular source of finance and may cause tensions.

In order to make up the £300,000 I think she should also take up the option of the bank loan at a fixed rate of interest of 6% per annum for 5 years. Furthermore, there is an offer of an overdraft. Sales are likely to be seasonal, particularly the toy shop, and so there may be times when she is short of cash and needs an overdraft.

In evaluation, I believe that raising finance in this way enables her to keep control. Once the bank loan is repaid after 5 years, her cousin's 50% ownership of the business may make it reasonable for him to receive 50% of the profits, especially considering the fact that he would have not received any profit from the first few years. Fàtima will only be paying £6,000 a year in the first 5 years on these three sources of finance. This will help her to establish the business.

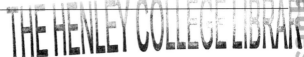

e This answer starts with a clear focus on the criteria that Fàtima should use when selecting the ways in which she raises finance. The remainder of the answer then follows logically. The conclusion is particularly strong, as it quantifies the costs of these types of finance for Fàtima, demonstrating the relatively low cost in the early years, while acknowledging potential problems in the long term.

(c) Both businesses have their strengths and weaknesses.

The computer store makes £40,000 profit and only needs 3,000 customers in order to break even. In contrast, the toy shop only makes £30,000 and needs 4,000 customers to break even.

For the computer business there is a margin of safety of 2,000 customers, but for the toy shop the margin of safety is higher at 2,500 customers.

If Fàtima is looking for profit, she should choose the computer store but if she is looking for a lower risk then the toy shop may be a better bet, as it has a larger margin of safety.

There are other issues to consider: she can get help from friends when it comes to running the computer shop. On the other hand, she knows less about computers and is more enthusiastic about the toy shop.

Fàtima needs to consider her quality of life. She would probably enjoy the toy shop more. There may also be hidden savings. How much does she pay for childminding at the moment? If it is possible for her children to stay in the toy shop (and this may not be an easy as she thinks), she may save money.

Finally, what are the long-term prospects for both businesses? Computer sales are increasing and toy sales appear to be falling. However, the computer shop is expected to be making a lot of money because she has a cheap supplier. It says in the case that this will not last for long. The loss of the major competition to the toy shop may mean that despite falling sales overall, in her town there may be scope for more sales in the toy shop.

On balance, I would advise Fàtima to choose the toy shop. It fits in with her interests and in the long term would probably make more money.

e Another excellent evaluative answer by candidate A.

Although candidate A showed poor examination technique in answering question 1(b), they only lost marks because of this in 1(b)(iv). The remaining answers are of an excellent standard and this script would receive a high grade A.

■ ■ ■

Answer to case study 4: candidate B

1 **(a)** An overdraft is a situation where a bank manager lets a person borrow money from the bank.

📝 Technically an overdraft is money borrowed from a bank. However, this answer seems to be explaining a bank loan, where a specific sum is borrowed, rather than an overdraft, where a person is allowed to spend more money than they have in their account.

(b) (i) It depends on the level of output.

📝 Candidate B has not read the question carefully and appears to be looking at variable costs. Always check the wording of the question.

(ii) total revenue – total costs at 5,000 units = £152,000 – £108,000 = £44,000

📝 Strictly speaking, the answer is £40,000, but candidate B would benefit from having clearly laid out their answer. A small margin of error is usually allowed when reading figures from a graph, so this answer would receive full marks.

(iii) The margin of safety is the difference between the breakeven output and the actual output.

📝 There is no attempt at a calculation but the formula would earn a mark.

(iv) total contribution = total revenue – total variable costs

At 5,000 units this is £150,000 – £50,000 = £100,000.

📝 An excellent answer that would earn full marks. The more usual way of calculating total contribution is: contribution per unit × no. of units = (£30 – £10) × 5,000 = £20 × 5,000 = £100,000. In a breakeven chart, this calculation is much more difficult because the selling price and variable cost per unit need to be worked out first. Candidate B has not only got the answer right but also saved time.

(c) breakeven output = $\dfrac{\text{fixed costs}}{\text{contribution per unit}}$

📝 This is the second occasion on which candidate B has remembered the formula, but not been able to apply it. Knowing the formulae is vital in this section of the specification, but it is much more likely that you will be asked to use the formulae in a calculation, so make sure that you get plenty of practice before the exam.

2 **(a)** Fátima could lower the breakeven output by marketing the toy shop more fully. This would attract more customers and enable her to make more profit.

She could also stock more games. These will attract more people into the shop and hopefully she will reach breakeven more easily.

🖉 Question 2(a) is a very specific question about lowering breakeven output. There are only three possible answers: increasing the selling price, lowering the fixed costs or lowering variable costs. Candidate B has assumed that anything that increases profits will lower breakeven output, but this is not the case. The suggestions presented here may well help the shop to make profits, but both of them would do so by bringing in more customers. In fact, they would both increase costs (marketing and stock), and therefore more customers, rather than fewer, would be needed in order to reach breakeven.

(b) I think that the first way of raising finance should be the venture capitalist, who has agreed to put in £100,000 and offer weekly advice to Fàtima in return for a 40% shareholding. This may seem to be a high shareholding, but £100,000 represents a third of the money in the company. With his excellent advice Fàtima's business is much more likely to succeed. The venture capitalist may also be able to give Fàtima useful business contacts that may help the business.

I would advise Fàtima to accept the offer from one of her friends, or perhaps she could get them to share the £100,000. This will still leave Fàtima with 38% of the shares. If she raised £200,000 this way it would only leave her with 16% of the shares. This does seem rather low for all the effort that she is making.

Finally, I would advise her to take the bank loan. According to the figures given, both businesses will be making a lot of profit from the beginning, so the bank loan could be repaid quite quickly. This will also have the advantage of keeping the £100,000 that Fàtima has saved, to be used in case of emergency.

🖉 Note how candidate B has suggested very different ways of raising the finance in comparison to candidate A. However, both candidates have justified their logic very effectively, so both would earn very high marks for their answers to this question. For evaluation questions there is not always one correct approach, so evaluation marks are awarded for the quality of the arguments presented by the candidate.

(c) Reasons for the computer shop:
- Fàtima has friends who can help her with technical advice.
- She has a cheap supplier who can help her to make a lot of money.

Reasons for the toy shop:
- Fàtima seems to be more interested in toys than computers.
- There is no close competition.

🖉 Don't use bullet points in this way. If you are running out of time towards the end of an exam, it is better to make a couple of points and explain them than make a list of separate points.

In places, candidate B is let down by a lack of application in his/her answers, but scored well on content/knowledge. Candidate B produced an excellent answer to question 2(b), which pulled the script up from a

U grade to a borderline C. Strong answers to these high-mark questions can make a major difference to your grade, as the final two questions — 2(b) and 2(c) — account for at least half of the marks awarded.

C5

Dave's Garden Centre

This case study focuses on 'Using cash-flow forecasting', 'Setting budgets' and 'Assessing business start-ups'.

Answer all questions   **Time allowed: 1 hour 15 minutes**

Read the case study below and then answer the questions that follow.

Dave was a very keen gardener and loved nothing better than spending his time tending plants in the garden. He loved the outdoor life. When some land on the outskirts of his village became available for rent, Dave seized the opportunity to set up a small garden centre.

Dave had become fed up with his job and wanted to earn more money — he felt that   5
running his own business would help him to achieve his aim of making £20,000 a year. He decided to get advice on the possible financial performance of a garden centre. An old school friend, Jim, had set up a garden centre of a similar size, about 50 miles away from Dave's proposed site. He was only too happy to give Dave some financial data in return for Dave's advice on some new roses and lilies.   10

In the absence of any other data, Dave decided that Jim's cash-flow forecast for his first year (Table 1) would be useful in order to forecast the finances of his own business.

	January to March	April to June	July to September	October to December
Opening balance (£s)	(i)	730	9,230	17,630
Quarterly inflows/ cash sales (£s)	14,000	24,000	21,400	17,300
Wages (£s)	4,400 ~~4,840~~	5,000 ~~2,500~~	5,000 ~~3,500~~	4,500 ~~4,950~~
Purchases of materials (£s)	4,200	7,000	(ii)	4,800
Other costs (£s)	14,000	3,500	1,900	2,700
Quarterly outflows (£s)	22,600	15,500	13,000	12,000
Net cash flow for quarter (£s)	(8,600)	8,500	8,400	5,300
Closing balance (£s)	730	9,230	17,630	22,930

Table 1 Forecast cash flow for the first year of trading of Jim's Garden Centre

Jim's Garden Centre was larger than Dave's and the data were a few years old. But allowing for inflation Dave reckoned that the cash-flow figures would be very helpful   15
in setting both his own cash-flow forecast and his budgets, especially as all of his transactions would be in cash.

All the same, Dave had no experience in running a business and had only decided to open a garden centre because gardening was his interest. He searched on the internet for information about garden centres and spoke to his bank manager, who introduced   20
him to a business adviser. The adviser was an excellent source of information as he specialised in rural businesses, such as garden centres. By the end of the week, Dave had compiled an income budget, an expenditure budget and a profit budget for the garden centre.

Dave had received some worrying information — raw material costs had been   25
increasing quite substantially. This was likely to cause his costs to rise much more rapidly than expected. The adviser also warned him that the area in which he was locating was well away from any main roads and that this might lead to delays in deliveries. Garden centres often suffered from unexpected changes in demand. If Dave chose the wrong plants to stock, he might suffer a dramatic decline in sales. Larger   30
garden centres were able to overcome this problem by stocking a complete range of plants and flowers.

Questions

1 (a) **What is meant by the term 'closing balance' (Table 1)?**   (2 marks)
   (b) (i) **What is the missing figure at (i) in the cash-flow forecast?**   (2 marks)
       (ii) **What is the missing figure at (ii) in the cash-flow forecast?**   (2 marks)
   (c) **Dave's cash-flow forecast is going to be identical to Jim's with only one exception: the wages Dave pays will be 10% higher than those paid by Jim in his cash flow. Based on this change, calculate Dave's closing balance at the end of his first year of trading.**   (5 marks)
   (d) **Identify three sources of information for a cash-flow forecast.**   (3 marks)
   (e) **Explain two possible objectives of Dave's business start-up.**   (6 marks)
2 (a) **Analyse two reasons why Dave would want to complete a cash-flow forecast.**   (10 marks)
   (b) **To what extent did Dave manage to overcome problems that he might have met in setting his budgets?**   (15 marks)
   (c) **Discuss the reasons why Dave's business might fail.**   (15 marks)

■ ■ ■

Answer to case study 5: candidate A

1 (a) It is the amount of cash held at the end of a particular period of time in the cash-flow forecast.

   ☑ A clear and concise definition that earns both marks.

   (b) (i)   £9,330
       (ii)   £6,100

   ☑ Two correct answers.

(c) Wages total £18,900. 10% = £1,890. Closing balance = £22,930 – £1,890 = £21,040.

18900

📝 Full marks are awarded for an efficient calulation.

(d) Other businesses, business advisers, market research.

📝 Three correct answers. The word 'identify' means that no explanation is required.

(e) Dave's main objective appears to be an enjoyable work experience outdoors. Dave was not enjoying his present job but loved gardening and the idea that he could earn money from this would be a main aim.

A secondary objective was to make money (£20,000). However, the business appeared to be expecting to make less than £20,000.

📝 These answers are explained well in the context of Dave's business.

2 (a) Firstly, Dave would want to see if he was likely to get into difficulties. If the forecast showed a shortage of money at any time, he could take steps to plan to raise finance, such as by getting an overdraft. Bank managers are always very keen to look at a cash-flow forecast before supporting a start-up business. Overall, the cash-flow forecast appears to indicate that this financial support is not needed. This is very useful information for Dave.

A cash-flow forecast can also help Dave to understand that his business will be seasonal and that cash flow may be reduced in the winter months. It also emphasises the relative difficulties of the opening of a new business — his net cash flow in the first quarter is expected to be negative.

📝 This is a strong answer that draws upon the case study in order to present two powerful reasons for compiling a cash-flow forecast.

(b) Dave was very inexperienced and this would have created problems for him in setting his budget. He was setting up from scratch and not using an existing business which might have had previous financial records.

Dave overcame these problems well. He contacted his friend, Jim, who had set up a garden centre, and persuaded him to give access to his cash-flow forecasts. Dave then recognised that there may be some amendments needed and made an adjustment for wage levels as a result of this.

Overall I feel that Dave faced many challenges in setting budgets but worked hard to overcome them. As a result it is probable that the budgets were as accurate as possible for a new business start-up.

📝 This answer shows an excellent blend of analysis and application, with answers that are built upon business logic and related well to Dave's Garden Centre. Although the overall evaluation at the end is quite brief, there are evaluative qualities in earlier paragraphs, such as the recognition that Jim's forecast may not be quite relevant to Dave's business in terms of wage levels.

(c) Dave had no experience in running a business and decided to open a garden centre because he loved gardening. A hobby is not necessarily the best reason to set up a business on which one is depending for a living.

Dave's research gave him some worrying information — raw material costs were likely to rise a lot. This would be likely to cause his costs to rise much more rapidly than expected. Garden centres are a luxury, so high prices might lead to garden centres suffering more than most other business.

Dave's business adviser warned him that the area in which he was locating was well away from any main roads and that this might lead to delays in deliveries. It would damage his reputation if customers expected to be able to buy plants that were not available. As it is in a remote area, customers may decide not to visit again if they've had a disappointing experience.

Finally, garden centres often experience unexpected changes in demand. The larger garden centres could overcome this problem by stocking a complete range of plants and flowers, but Dave would have to hope that he had chosen his stock correctly.

The remoteness of Dave's Garden Centre and the limited stock that he can possess is likely to be the main reason why the business might fail. However, this needs to be set against Dave's enthusiasm, his careful planning and good information sources, and the fact that his financial forecasts appeared to indicate positive outcome.

🖉 This is an excellent approach to this question. Candidate A has presented potential reasons for failure and applied them to Dave's business, concluding that the strengths may mean that the business will not fail.

Candidate A would earn high marks on every question and would achieve a strong A grade in this paper.

case study

6

Sticky Buns

This case study integrates all of the elements of the Unit 1 specification.

Answer all questions   **Time allowed: 1 hour 15 minutes**

Read the case study below and then answer the questions that follow.

Ellie loved sticky buns. When her children were old enough to go to school she opened a bakery called 'Sticky Buns', specialising in cakes. A number of customers observed that they enjoyed the freshly baked cakes, so Ellie converted the old stock room into a small restaurant serving drinks and snacks. Her speciality was sticky buns made to order. On entering the shop, the customer would select a type of bun and choose from 5 one of 50 different flavours of icing and, if required, an additional topping such as a chocolate flake.

The original idea had come from a brainstorming session with some friends. Further changes were made as a result of some qualitative market research among customers, mainly from a focus group that met on Wednesday evenings. 10

Most bakery products had relatively low levels of added value, but the sticky buns and restaurant were an exception. After the first year of trading, Ellie wanted to know if the restaurant was making a profit, so she looked at some financial data. The data are shown in Table 1.

Average spend per customer	£4.50
Average variable cost per customer	£1.00
Fixed costs per month	£1,820
Expected number of customers per month	900

Table 1 Financial data related to the first year of Ellie's restaurant

Before becoming an entrepreneur Ellie had not enjoyed life as an employee. She 15 wanted to be her own boss, particularly as this would give her control of her working hours. She intended to fit her job around her children's school hours, although she also wanted to make a reasonable profit. Most important was the attraction of doing something that she had enjoyed all her life — baking bread and cakes. Pursuing her hobby was a dream come true for Ellie, who was also looking forward to interacting 20 with customers — her previous job at a call centre had not given her this opportunity and Ellie considered herself to be a sociable person.

At first Ellie was the only worker, but as the business grew she started to employ some part-time staff. These were mostly college students who were prepared to accept the minimum wage, but there was a high turnover of part-time staff as the students 25 left for better-paid jobs or moved on to university. Other part-time staff tended to grab opportunities of full-time positions when they arose in other businesses. Overall, her part-time staff proved to be quite unreliable and Ellie was often left short of staff because of supposed illnesses among the part-time staff. After 3 years, Ellie decided to change her policy and started to employ full-time employees. Immediately she found them to be much more committed, less likely to be absent and more willing to take greater responsibility, although this may have been because of the higher wages she had to pay in order to recruit them. Unfortunately, full-time staff preferred working Mondays to Fridays. Although the bakery was always busy during the week, the restaurant served over 60% of its customers on Saturdays and Sundays. However, full-time staff were reluctant to work at weekends in comparison to part-time staff and sometimes Ellie found herself short of staff, with queues of irate customers. 30 35

Despite her staffing difficulties, Ellie decided to open up a new bakery and restaurant in a neighbouring town. The reputation of 'Sticky Buns' had spread and the bank manager was impressed with the business plan and the financial predictions. However, he was concerned that Ellie was trying to finance the business herself and had turned down offers from venture capitalists because she had not wanted them to take any control away from her ownership. The bank manager was also concerned that Ellie was still trading as a sole trader. He explained: 'In catering there is always a risk of accidents that could lead to a court case and a large debt. Furthermore, you have quite high fixed costs and if you lost customers you could end up making a big financial loss. I would advise you to become a private limited company and offer some venture capitalists a 50% share of your business in return for the capital that you need to open your new bakery and restaurant.' 40 45

Questions

1 (a) **What is meant by the term 'brainstorming' (line 8)?** (2 marks)
   (b) **What is meant by 'qualitative market research' (line 9)** (3 marks)
   (c) **Using the data in the article, calculate the number of customers per month that Ellie needs for her restaurant to break even.** (5 marks)
   (d) **Calculate the monthly profit or loss for Ellie's restaurant.** (4 marks)
   (e) **Outline two reasons why Ellie's sticky buns are able to add value to a greater extent than her other bakery products.** (6 marks)
2 (a) **Analyse the main motives that led to Ellie becoming an entrepreneur.** (10 marks)
   (b) **Discuss the merits of Ellie's decision to move from employing just part-time staff to employing only full-time staff.** (14 marks)
   (c) **Ellie's bank manager said: 'I would advise you to become a private limited company and offer some venture capitalists a 50% share of your business in return for the capital that you need to open your new bakery and restaurant.' Do you agree with his advice? Justify your view.** (16 marks)

■ ■ ■

Answer to case study 6: candidate A

1 (a) Brainstorming is a technique whereby a group of people try to generate as many ideas as possible in order to solve a particular problem. The best solution is then determined by subsequent analysis of the list of ideas.

> This is an excellent definition, showing full understanding of the concept of brainstorming. Given the fact that there were 2 marks to be awarded for this definition, the first sentence would have been sufficient to secure both marks. However, some definition questions will have a maximum of 3 marks because a more detailed definition is either appropriate or required. If this question had been a 3-mark definition question, the examiner would have been expecting slightly more than the first sentence. In this instance, the further clarification provided by the second sentence would have secured all 3 marks.

(b) Qualitative market research is when customers or potential customers are asked for their opinion. It focuses on factors such as the reasons why a product is bought or why people prefer a product, rather than looking at numerical information showing how many people buy certain products. In Ellie's case, the qualitative market research took place in the Wednesday evening focus group.

> Another excellent definition. The second sentence is particularly strong, as it shows that the candidate understands what is meant by an opinion; this is critical to the definition of qualitative market research. Further clarification of the concept is shown in the contrast with numerical information (quantitative market research) in the second part of the second sentence. The final sentence confirms the excellent understanding of the candidate, by providing an example that is relevant to the case. In many cases, this example is crucial to candidates whose definitions may be vague. In this case, however, it would have added no further marks as full marks would have been received much earlier in the answer.

(c) The number of customers that Ellie requires in order to break even is:

$$\frac{\text{fixed costs per month}}{\text{contribution per customer}} = \frac{£1,890}{£3.50} = 540 \text{ customers}$$

> This answer is incorrect but it still receives 4 of the 5 marks available. The candidate clearly understands the formula for calculating the breakeven number of customers, but has inadvertently put in a wrong figure for fixed costs. Almost certainly this was just an error in transcribing the figure from the article. If the candidate had divided £1,820 by £3.50, they would have received full marks. The bottom part of the fraction — contribution per customer — is understood because £3.50 is the correct calculation from subtracting £1 from £4.50. However, it is good practice to show all the working because if the subtraction had been carried out incorrectly, no credit could have been given for understanding contribution per unit.

Because the candidate has carried out a calculation correctly, making only a minor copying error, only 1 mark has been lost. It should be noted that if the candidate had carried out this calculation on a rough piece of paper and had just put the answer (540 customers) into their answer book, they would have received zero marks. This is because the examiner would not have been able to see any understanding. It is vital that working out is shown in the exam paper itself, so that credit can be awarded for parts of a calculation that are correct.

(d) The monthly profit for Ellie's restaurant is:

(number of customers − breakeven number of customers) × contribution per customer = (900 − 540) × £3.50 = 360 × £3.50 = £1,260

Although not the normal method of calculating profit, it is an acceptable approach and is a more efficient way of calculating profit if the breakeven output has already been calculated. Once the fixed costs have been paid, every customer above the breakeven quantity is contributing towards profit. The candidate shows that the first 540 customers contributed towards paying off the fixed costs. This leaves the remaining 360 customers to contribute towards profit. They each contribute £3.50, giving a total profit of 360 x £3.50 = £1,260.

Unfortunately, this is the wrong answer, because the candidate incorrectly calculated the breakeven quantity in question 1(c). In these situations the examination boards follow a policy known as the 'own figure rule' (OFR). A candidate must not be penalised twice for the same mistake. Candidate A has already been penalised in question 1(c), so in question 1(d) the candidate's breakeven output of 540 is accepted as correct and the answer marked accordingly. Therefore this answer receives full marks because it is the profit that would have been made if 540 had been the breakeven output. Once again, this shows the importance of showing your working out. If this candidate had merely put the answer of £1,260, the examiner would have had no way of knowing that they understood how to calculate profit and would have given no marks to this answer.

By showing their working out this candidate received a total of 8 out of 9 marks for questions 1(c) and 1(d). If no working out had been shown, they would have received zero marks for the two answers given.

(e) Added value is the difference between the selling price of a product and the cost of bought-in goods and services. Ellie's sticky buns are able to add value because they are unique. A customer in a supermarket will be faced with a limited choice of buns, but in Ellie's bakery they are able to acquire the bun that they like with the icing of their preference. Furthermore, their satisfaction can be increased even more by a topping that would not be available in a supermarket. All of these factors combine to give great satisfaction to the customer and so it will persuade them to pay a much higher price. The icing and toppings will not cost Ellie very much, so there will be a large difference between the selling price and the cost of bought-in goods and services.

e The question asked for two reasons, but this response focuses on only one reason. Despite this limitation the answer would still score very highly. Content marks are awarded both for definitions of the term in the question and, in this case, statement of the reason(s) for adding value. With one reason and a very clear understanding of adding value, this candidate would secure all of the content marks. Application skills are also very good, although they have been limited by the focus on only one reason. Consequently, maximum marks for application would not quite be reached.

It should be noted that 6-mark questions asking for two reasons/factors do not award up to 3 marks for each factor. It is possible to earn up to 5 marks for an excellent answer that focuses on just one factor, although higher marks are more likely if two factors are discussed.

2 (a) There were lots of reasons for Ellie wanting to become an entrepreneur. The main ones were:

- Ellie had not enjoyed life as an employee.
- She wanted to be her own boss.
- She wanted to fit her job around her children's school hours.
- She wanted to make a profit.
- She wanted to do something that she enjoyed.
- She wanted an opportunity to meet people.

e This is an example of poor examination technique. The use of bullet points should be avoided, as they encourage brief answers that tend to lack application and analysis. In addition, too many separate points are being made in this answer. Typically, you will be expected to provide two or three arguments for a 10-mark question. The expectation is that these arguments should focus in detail on the reasons for Ellie becoming an entrepreneur. Candidate A has not done this and would have earned content marks for noting down some valid reasons but no further marks for application and analysis, because no explanations are provided.

(b) Should Ellie have employed just full-time or part-time staff? I believe that she should not have concentrated on just one type of staff.

Part-time staff provide certain benefits, as indicated in the case study, but they also caused her a number of problems. Eventually she decided to move on to full-time staff. With just full-time staff she suffered different problems but gained from some alternative benefits.

My advice to Ellie is that she should employ a mixture of full-time and part-time staff so that she can get the best of both worlds. For example, the part-time staff will work for a lower hourly wage rate and this will save Ellie money.

e This is an unusual approach to the question. Initially the candidate has gone straight into a conclusion. Although this may seem to be answering the question, conclusions are much more forceful at the end of an argument or answer when the examiner can see whether the evaluation has been produced as a result of logical reasoning.

The most unusual aspect of this answer is the fact that the candidate has focused almost solely on the words 'just' and 'only', rather than the expected focus on full-time and part-time staff. Because these words are a relevant part of the question, any arguments presented will be credited, if appropriate. Unfortunately, candidate A presents a very vague response, with mentions of problems and benefits that are never specified. If specific references had been noted and explained, this could have been a good answer. However, as they were not explained it was not possible to reward this answer until the very final sentence, where one specific benefit of using part-time employees is shown. Even then it was not explained, so this answer would have received just one content mark. The examiner would have noted the evaluation or judgement made in the opening sentence and gone back to see if there was supporting evidence for this judgement in the rest of the answer. In this case the answer was 'no' and so evaluation would not have been credited.

(c) Ellie has put a lot of hard work into establishing her business. It is probable that her new restaurant will be more successful than her original bakery because she has already established a good reputation in the local area.

To some extent the success of the new bakery will depend on how close to the original bakery the new restaurant is. If it is too far away, the reputation of Sticky Buns may not be known. Also it will be much harder for Ellie to manage the new restaurant if it is a long way away. She seems to have been very much a hands-on manager in all aspects of the first Sticky Buns shop, so she may not be good at controlling a new shop from a long distance.

There is no evidence to suggest that Ellie has got any patents on Sticky Buns and, as her buns are based on other bakery products, it is likely that she would not be allowed to get any patents. Therefore she has no protection against competition stealing her ideas. In situations like this it is best to expand as quickly as possible to stop competition using your ideas. This suggests that Ellie should be trying to grow as quickly as possible. With her own financial target being a reasonable profit I imagine that she has not made enough money to open up a new store. For this reason I think she should take the bank manager's advice to get financial help from outside.

A greater priority for Ellie is to become a private limited company. If she is still a sole trader then she has unlimited liability and can be held responsible for all of the debts of her business. As her bank manager says: 'In catering there is always a risk of accidents that could lead to a court case and a large debt.' If something like this happened to Ellie's business, she would lose all of her personal possessions, possibly even the family home. For this reason she must get limited liability. She could open up a private limited company with her husband or a friend if she did not wish to get involved with venture capitalists.

Looking at the list of original reasons for Ellie becoming an entrepreneur, I do not think she should set up a new restaurant in a different town. Ellie intended to fit her job around her children's school hours and unless they have now grown up it is difficult to see how she can do this whilst running a business in a different town. As she moves from owner to manager she will also find that she has less interaction with customers and almost certainly she will be leaving the baking to her employees.

Unless Ellie's priorities have changed considerably, my advice to her is to become a private limited company, in case of sudden debts, but not to open up a new restaurant in a neighbouring town. Therefore she will not need any help from venture capitalists.

⌐℮ This is an excellent answer. It covers a number of relevant ideas, and as each idea is developed there is a suggestion of judgement/evaluation within the body of the answer. Another particular strength of this answer is its application. Each of the arguments being presented is linked very closely to the article, so while candidate A is developing a line of argument (analysis), they are also ensuring that this analysis is being presented in the context of the business (application). This answer would have received full marks.

Overall, candidate A showed all of the qualities of an A-grade candidate throughout question 1 and also in question 2(c). Unfortunately, the answers to 2(a) and 2(b) were U-grade responses. As these are heavily weighted questions, representing just over a quarter of the total marks awarded, candidate A would have fallen short of an overall grade A. Consistency throughout an examination is a great advantage. However, because of the excellence of most of candidate A's answers, they would still have been close to an A grade and would have secured enough marks to earn a very comfortable B grade.

■ ■ ■

Answer to case study 6: candidate B

1 (a) I do not know what brainstorming is but I guess that it is something about trying to come up with a storm — lots of ideas, using your brain.

⌐℮ It is not wise to tell the examiner that you do not know the answer to a question! The answer does suggest that the candidate is guessing, but it shows some understanding of the concept of brainstorming, even if it was a lucky guess. This answer would have earned 1 mark.

If you have a vague idea, it is always worth a guess unless you believe that it will lead to you running out of time. A blank answer is guaranteed to score zero marks; a guess may earn a mark. There is nothing to lose except the time it takes to write your answer.

(b) Qualitative market research is about finding out from potential customers whether they would buy a product. Primary market research is qualitative.

☒ This answer is too vague. Both qualitative and quantitative market research are intended to discover whether potential customers will buy a product, so a little more clarity is needed to distinguish between them. The second sentence is also misleading, as although qualitative market research tends to be primary, it is not necessarily true that primary market research will be qualitative, as it can be both qualitative and quantitative.

It is important to ensure that your definition clearly distinguishes the concept in the question from any similar concepts.

There is enough substance in this answer to gain limited credit, but in contrast to 1(a), where candidate B appears to have been lucky, in 1(b) there is a suggestion that candidate B knows more than they are saying.

(c)

Output	Total revenue	Total costs	Profit
900	4,050	2,720	1,330
800	3,600	2,620	980
700	3,150	2,520	630
600	2,700	2,420	280
500	2,250	2,320	(70)
525	2,362.50	2,345	17.50
520	2,340	2,340	0

The breakeven quantity is 520 customers per month.

☒ This is the correct answer and so it would earn full marks. Although it is expected that candidates will use the formula to calculate the breakeven output, any method that leads to the correct answer is acceptable. However, caution should be taken before adopting 'trial and error' in a calculation of this sort. Although the detailed calculations are not shown (it is always advisable to show working), these calculations must have taken a long time. Candidate B would earn all 5 marks for this calculation, but it is likely that they will be penalised by running out of time on other questions. In these situations, it is best to move on and return to a question **if** there is time remaining towards the end of the exam.

(d) The monthly profit from 900 customers is £1,330.

☒ The 'inappropriate' method employed when answering question 1(c) may not have been such an issue for candidate B, as it has given them the answer to 1(d) in the opening line of their table. This answer is correct and would earn full marks. It is possible that candidate B was aware that the table used in 1(c) would lead to both questions being answered.

(e) The sticky buns are able to add value more because people will pay more for them because the ingredients are more costly. It is easier to make bread and so the profit will be lower on bread as there will be more competitors making bread.

e It is evident that candidate B can think logically, but their responses are being hampered by the lack of clarity in their understanding of key terms. The first sentence indicates a lack of understanding, but the second sentence earns some credit for linking added value to the level of competition, which is an important factor that influences how much value can be added.

2 (a) There were a number of motives behind Ellie wanting to become an entrepreneur.

Ellie had not enjoyed being an employee, so she was determined to be her own boss. This seemed to be the main motivator as there did not appear to be too much of a need for her to make money. However, as with most entrepreneurs she wanted to make a profit.

Most importantly, Ellie wanted to meet people whilst doing something that she enjoyed. Running 'Sticky Buns' was ideal for these purposes. She loved the creativity of baking and was able to earn some money for the family from doing this. Almost certainly she would have enjoyed the opportunity to socialise, as a bakery/restaurant is the sort of place where you could chat. The number of customers per month suggests that she was not too busy and would have been able to socialise with customers. The profit (£1,330 per month) may not have been very good, but this might be because the shop had limited opening hours so that she could fit it around her children's school hours.

e For analysis questions, it is usually advisable to focus on two, possibly three, factors and develop them in detail. This answer is unusual in that it combines a wide range of motives, but integrates them in a way that reveals an excellent insight into Ellie's motives. The observation concerning the number of customers and the potential link to Ellie meeting her social needs is particularly strong, as is the recognition that the profit may be less significant than the need to fit the business around her children. There is evaluation in this response, and although there are no specific marks for evaluation, candidate B's approach to this question would earn full marks for both application and analysis.

(b) Full-time staff depend on their job for their living. They are more motivated than part-timers, who may have other priorities.

e The answer introduces a valid line of argument but then moves on to a separate point without explaining the reasoning behind the argument. There is no attempt to apply the answer to 'Sticky Buns'.

(c) A private limited company (plc) is owned by shareholders and will mean more money for the business.

Venture capitalists take shares in a business in return for providing capital.

e Candidate B makes a common mistake — confusing private limited companies (ltds) with public limited companies (plcs). Ensure that you are aware of the difference! The second sentence earns no credit because it is copied directly from the question and is not giving any further information on venture capitalists.

The answers to the final two questions suggest that candidate B was running out of time at the end of the examination. This is almost certainly a result of the poor examination technique shown in spending too much time on question 1(c). Remember 'a mark a minute': if an answer takes a lot longer than this, it may put you under pressure elsewhere. Candidate B shows some calculation skills and is able to develop a sound line of argument, as shown in the answer to question 2(a). However, they have been let down by poor understanding of definitions. Most of the marks earned by candidate B were on the calculation questions and question 2(a), which was not based on knowing a key term. A further example of weak exam technique is shown by the brevity of the answers to questions 2(b) and 2(c). These two questions have been completed in just a few lines and yet they account for 50% of the marks. These issues have led to a script that would earn a D grade, despite candidate B completing three questions that would earn full marks.